I0801889

Praise for
Hear Today

"Fiensy's treatment of each of the twelve selected parables of Jesus is unparalleled in clarity and relevance. Not only are his explanations biblically accurate, they are applied with precision to our personal struggles, and the applications are vividly illustrated from actual examples drawn from today's headlines. While written for small group study, *Hear Today* is a can't-miss resource for teaching and preaching the parables in a way that is sure to connect with the human heart."

—**Keith P. Keeran,** Chancellor and Distinguished Professor of Leadership and Communication, Kentucky Christian University

"With considerable scholarly knowledge of first-century society and culture, David Fiensy interfaces deft understanding of the parables with contemporary awareness and insight. This very readable volume will enhance personal devotions, enrich small groups, and bless countless other church audiences."

—**William R. Baker,** Editor, *Stone-Campbell Journal*

"It is a rarity to find an individual with the mind of a scholar and the heart of a pastor, but David Fiensy is such a man. His *Hear Today* is an insightful resource for small groups to delve into the parables of Jesus beyond the common devotional, surface-level engagement of the text. Fiensy brings the insights of scholarship on the parables into the practical context of a small group study, and the results are beneficial for anyone at every stage of life. I would encourage any small group to spend a season studying the parables of Jesus through *Hear Today*."

—**James Estep,** Vice President of Academics, Central Christian College of the Bible, Missouri

"*Hear Today* is creative, informative, historical, and contemporary. With stories to help the reader listen even as they read, Fiensy explains the parables in a way to see application for one's life today. Fiensy's approach to these parables will make one think and then act!"

—**Joe Grana II,** Dean of Pacific Christian College of Bible and Ministry Studies, Hope International University

"Wow! What a stirring, fresh approach to Jesus's parables using contemporary settings and applications. Every pastor, youth pastor, and Christian teacher will find a wealth of well-researched and illustrated material in *Hear Today* for sermons, lessons, and devotions."

—**Rob Ford,** Professor Emeritus, Kentucky Christian University

"Information. Inspiration. Application. David has taken some of the most thought-provoking lessons Jesus ever taught and provided practical insight alongside biblical truth. This book brings the parables of Jesus to life and places them in our modern, complex world. I highly recommend you sit with this book and let it move you closer to the heart of Jesus."

—**Jason Cullum,** lead pastor, Christ's Church, Jacksonville, Florida

"The current climate in New Testament scholarship is that the parables of Jesus have multiple meanings, making it difficult for those interested to ascertain the original intent of Jesus's enigmatic stories. Fiensy puts a lifetime of scholarship to work to discover both the original intent of these parables and their practical relevance. A churchman at heart, Fiensy is concerned not to let the trees obscure the forest. He works through the parables gently and shrewdly, articulating their place in the teaching of Jesus and in the Kingdom life of the modern church."

—**Les Hardin,** Professor of New Testament, Johnson University, Florida

"*Hear Today* is a gem! Fiensy writes with clarity and gives fresh perspective on the application of some of Jesus's parables. His retelling of the parables is compelling and impresses on the reader the practical application we all can and should get from these stories. Questions at the end of each chapter make this a good book for group discussion or just personal reflection."

—**Cindy Willison,** Executive Assistant, Southland Christian Church, Lexington, Kentucky

HEAR
TODAY

HEAR TODAY

COMPASSION *and* GRACE IN THE **PARABLES** *of* JESUS

DAVID A. FIENSY

LEAFWOOD
PUBLISHERS
an imprint of Abilene Christian University Press

HEAR TODAY

Compassion and Grace in the Parables of Jesus

LEAFWOOD
PUBLISHERS
an imprint of Abilene Christian University Press

ISBN 978-1-68426-181-9 | LCCN 2020025841

Printed in the United States of America

LIBRARY OF CONGRESS CATALOGING-IN-PUBLICATION DATA
Names: Fiensy, David A., author.
Title: Hear today : compassion and grace in the parables of Jesus / David A. Fiensy.
Description: Abilene, Texas : Leafwood Publishers, 2021. | Includes bibliographical references.
Identifiers: LCCN 2020025841 (print) | LCCN 2020025842 (ebook) | ISBN 9781684261819 (paperback) | ISBN 9781684269433 (ebook)
Subjects: LCSH: Jesus Christ—Parables.
Classification: LCC BT375.3 .F64 2021 (print) | LCC BT375.3 (ebook) | DDC 226.8/06—dc23
LC record available at https://lccn.loc.gov/2020025841
LC ebook record available at https://lccn.loc.gov/2020025842

Cover design by ThinkPen Design, LLC | Interior text design by Strong Design, Sandy Armstrong

Leafwood Publishers is an imprint of Abilene Christian University Press
ACU Box 29138, Abilene, Texas 79699

1-877-816-4455 | www.leafwoodpublishers.com

21 22 23 24 25 26 / 7 6 5 4 3 2 1

To the churches at which I have preached over the past four decades (in alphabetical order): Browns Christian Church in Browns, Illinois; Carter Christian Church in Carter, Kentucky; Grape Grove Church of Christ in Jamestown, Ohio; and Monterey Christian Church in Batavia, Ohio. They were a blessing to me and my family.

CONTENTS

ACKNOWLEDGMENT

Thank you to my brother, Chris Fiensy, for kindly reading and editing this manuscript in its initial stages. His helpful insights have made it a better message.

INTRODUCTION TO THE PARABLES

When my kids were little, I wanted to teach them Christian ethics. I wanted them to grow up viewing the world as Jesus-followers. Little ones do not sit still for long lectures or sermons. So, what to do? I told them stories, stories with moral points to them. Oh, I embellished them, hammed it up, made them funny at certain points. But I also tried to instill a sensitivity for people, a heart of compassion, and a love for God. That way, they could enjoy the experience but also gradually absorb the message. Now, I wonder where I ever got the idea to teach theology by telling stories?

The word *parable* means something "thrown alongside" for comparison. It is an illustration, like a sermon illustration, that seeks to clarify a theological idea. There are many such stories in the Old Testament.[1] The rabbis of Jesus's day and later also loved using parables to explain ethical and theological concepts.[2] I will give examples of the rabbinic parables later in connection with some of Jesus's parables discussed in this book. The point is, Jesus inherited, from the Old Testament, the practice of telling stories to explain theological or ethical concepts. Jesus was at home in the Jewish world when he taught in parables.

Several interpreters have tried to be definitive in their explanation of what a parable is and does. One definition says: "A parable . . . employs a short narrative fiction to reference a transcendent symbol."[3] Milo Connick essentially said the same thing in more accessible language: "A parable is an earthly story with a heavenly meaning."[4] His expression has become a sort of standard in churches. Either way, we get the idea.[5] These stories—which may be actual events or entirely fictional—are meant to illustrate difficult ideas.

We might say a word about what parables are *not*. They are not fables—that is, stories in which animals or plants have speaking parts. The classic collection of ancient fables is Aesop's Greek Fables. In these tales, foxes, for example, speak and think. There are lessons from the animals and plants. There is one such story in the Bible. Jotham's fable (Judg. 9:6–21) has plants acting like human beings, making decisions and speaking. But none of Jesus's parables is like that.

Jesus's parables are also not allegories in the strict sense. An allegory is a story in which its several points refer to other events, persons, or ideas. Jesus's parables certainly have allegorical elements at times (the characters or items do refer to spiritual lessons), but we should be cautious about interpreting them "allegorically." In the medieval period, the church engaged in regular allegorical interpretation of Scripture, especially of the parables. The Parable of the Good Samaritan offers us an example. In this parable, a man travels from Jerusalem to Jericho, falls among bandits, is robbed and beaten, is ignored by a priest and a Levite, and is finally helped by a Samaritan who takes him to an inn and pays for his stay there. You will see how I interpret and apply this parable in Chapter

Eleven of this book, but here is how the famous theologian and Bible interpreter Augustine (AD 354–430) deciphers it:

> The man who went down to Jericho from Jerusalem represents Adam; Jerusalem is the city of peace from which Adam has fallen; Jericho represents mortality; the priest and Levite are the Old Testament era; the Samaritan represents Christ; the devil and his demons are the bandits; the inn in which the beaten man was housed is the church; the innkeeper is Paul.[6]

The allegorical interpretation of the Parable of the Good Samaritan is kind of neat; it has a certain appeal. But I really do not think this was Jesus's point. Jesus told this story in response to the question, "Who is my neighbor?" This question in turn was in response to Jesus's teaching that the second of the great commandments was to love your neighbor as yourself. Going into a heavy doctrinal statement told in allegorical form does not fit this context.

Nonetheless, there are two times in which Jesus himself gives a rather allegorical interpretation of his parables (see Chapters Five and Seven). In this case, we are certainly justified in the allegorical interpretation. It is given to us in the Scripture itself. Allegory was known in first-century Judaism. But I am cautious about interpreting the Bible freely that way. I think it can hide rather than clarify the Bible's meaning.

Some of the stories Jesus acquired from the culture of his day. There are stories in the Jewish literature very similar to what he told—but often with an important theological difference. Evidently, he took some of those little narratives and edited them for his own sermon illustrations. Other stories probably happened in a local village or somewhere in Palestine, and everyone knew about them. Jesus may have heard such stories growing up or in his pre-ministry travels as a carpenter and stored them in his memory for use later during his ministry. Still others he probably entirely created out of thin air. They are illustrations drawn from everyday experiences but not necessarily actual events and not already circulating within the culture. I think Jesus was a very creative storyteller—a master storyteller—and could generate narratives on the spot. Others, he may have thought about for some time until he got them just right. And, I would presume, he did not tell these parables only once. Common sense would demand that he recycled them again and again from village to village as he taught and preached, adapting and editing them slightly every time to fit the location and occasion.

Nor should we think that we have the parables exactly as Jesus told them. What I mean is, I think some of these parables took many minutes—even hours—to tell. I think Jesus could hold an audience spellbound for a long time, engrossed in the story, to press his theological message. These are fascinating tales, and one could see making them into whole movies today. Even the summaries we have are often dramatic and moving. To tell such stories in only the time it takes us today to read them (no longer than five minutes for any of them) would be unsatisfactory to Palestinian villagers with plenty of time on their hands and a vivid imagination hungering for entertainment. I can imagine the Parable of the Prodigal Son, for example (Chapter One), taking several hours to tell. There would have been many more details about the son's insult of his father, his flight to the "far country," what the far country was like (very pagan), his life of sin and debauchery, his downfall and hard times, and his return. The details are given to us in hints in the recorded parable, but I really do not think Jesus told such an abbreviated version. Remember, telling stories was the entertainment of a village. And if you had a skilled storyteller with many interesting tales, you would listen for hours.

And I can imagine Jesus's storytelling skills. The ancient orators often used different voices when they told such stories, even used painted pictures as visual aids. Did Jesus do the same? Why not? The fact that the summaries we have in the Gospels are so captivating means that when Jesus told them, they must have been even more interesting. This insight may help the reader to engage in the parables. When you read this book, I hope you will discuss it in a group. If so, assign reading parts to members of your group and dramatize the parables. Have someone be the father, someone be the younger son, someone else be the older son, and another person be one of the servants in the Parable of the Prodigal Son (Chapter One). I think you will get a new experience in reading the Bible.

Jesus's narratives were, at first perhaps, entertainment. Afterward, they became controversial, even troubling for some. And that was the intention. Jesus planted a seed of teaching which grew over time.

Here is the mystery of the parables of Jesus: Sometimes they do not clarify ideas but sort of hide them. They are difficult to interpret unless one has the key of the Christian gospel. The aim was to cause persons to have to think about the story until the point finally dawned on them. The effect would be more profound in that way. So, sometimes, when we read a parable, we say to ourselves, "The point is obvious." But, to the audience at that time, it was not. And it just may be that sometimes, although the point seems obvious to us, we are off the mark. Perhaps in the following chapters I will be able to convince you of slightly different understandings of some of your most familiar parables.

Klyne Snodgrass comments on Søren Kierkegaard's[7] thinking concerning communication and its application to the study of parables. Some communication is direct, such as that giving out simple teaching: "Do not steal." But other communication is indirect. Indirect communication "finds a way in a back window and confronts what one thinks is reality." So, instead of saying "do not steal," one could tell a story about a time when a man noticed a cash register drawer open and stealthily put a hundred-dollar bill into his pocket. He then went on to have certain bad experiences. We would then be left with our thoughts about the consequences of theft. Parables are indirect communication, writes Snodgrass.[8] They come in the back window of our minds and nudge us to certain conclusions and behaviors.

There is also a personal or existential side to the parables. They are like poems, not because they rhyme or have rhythm but because they excite our imagination. They are poetic in the sense that great literature speaks to us in different ways, depending on our situation at the time, our culture, and our general understanding of the Scriptures. It's like when two friends see a movie and one friend thinks the movie is "Okay, but not special," but the other is deeply moved by the experience. Why the difference? Because of what the second friend was going through at the time. In that sense, the parables are like multifaceted gems or jewels. You can turn them and turn them to see several different messages and applications. You might see one message at a certain point in your life—perhaps at a critical point or during a time of suffering—and an additional message at another point. Again, Snodgrass describes parables as Rorschach tests.[9] The inkblots say different things to different persons, depending on their current circumstances. My hope is that the discussions of the twelve parables highlighted in this book will increase your ability to see multiple applications to your own life story and will open you to let the parables speak to you in new ways.

Because Jesus tended to both hide and reveal in these stories, he often gave the challenge, "Whoever has ears to hear, let him [or her] hear" (Matt. 11:15; 13:9; 13:43; Mark 4:9; 4:23; 7:16;

Luke 8:8; 14:35). Or, as I have paraphrased it in the title to this study, *Hear Today*. In other words, pay attention. This will require some thought, some investment of your time, and some spiritual discernment. It is my hope that I can help you, the reader, think through twelve of Jesus's most famous and powerful parables, that I can help you "hear today."

How many parables are there in the four Gospels? Bible interpreters disagree somewhat on this answer. It all depends on how precisely one defines a parable. Some parables are in three Gospels, others in two, and many in only one Gospel. Most of the very short parables—one sentence in many cases—are in Matthew. On the other hand, Luke has some of the longest parables in the New Testament. Some think there are no parables in the Gospel of John at all. Others, defining the term parable more loosely, find a couple.

Luke's parables have plots, scene changes, and dialogue. They are truly engaging narratives. As I mentioned above, I think some of Luke's stories took Jesus hours to tell. Why not? They are great stories, inspiring stories. I can see him in the village square at night, scores of eyes—large and small—locked on him as he narrates some of the most significant narratives in history.

What follows in Table I.1 is, I think, a fair listing of all the parables in the four Gospels, though some might want to disagree here and there.[10]

Table I.1: Jesus's Parables

Parables Appearing in Three Gospels			
	Matthew	Mark	Luke
Salt of the Earth	5:13	9:50	14:34–35
Light of the World	5:15	4:21	8:16
Physician and Sick	9:12	2:17	5:31
Wedding Guests	9:15	2:19–20	5:34–35

New Cloth	9:16	2:21	5:36
New Wine	9:17	2:22	5:37–39
Sower*	13:3–9	4:3–9	8:5–8
Mustard Seed	13:31–32	4:30–32	13:18–19
Wicked Husbandmen	21:33–46	12:1–12	20:9–19
Fig Tree	24:32	13:28	21:29–30

Parables Appearing in Two Gospels		
	Matthew	**Luke**
The Accuser	5:25–26	12:58–59
The Lamp and the Body	6:22–23	11:34–35
Speck and Log	7:3–5	6:41–42
Tree and Fruit	7:16–20	6:43–45
House on the Rock	7:24–27	6:47–49
Children in the Marketplace	11:16–17	7:31–32
Return of the Evil Spirit	12:43–45	11:24–26
Leaven	13:33	13:20–21
Blind Guides	15:14	6:39
Signs	16:2–3	12:54–56
Lost Sheep	18:12–14	15:3–7
Faithful Servant	24:45–51	12:42–46
The Pounds/Talents*	25:14–30	19:11–27
Great Supper*	22:1–14	14:15–24

Parables Appearing in Only One Gospel	
Matthew	
City on a Hill	5:14
Wheat and Weeds*	13:24–30 (37–43)
Hidden Treasure	13:44
The Pearl	13:45–46
The Net	13:47–48

The Householder	13:52
Unforgiving Servant*	18:23–34
Laborers in the Vineyard*	20:1–15
Two Sons	21:28–31
Wedding Garment	22:11–13
Ten Virgins	25:1–13
Sheep and Goats	25:31–46
Mark	
Seed Growing Secretly	4:26–29
Watchful Doorkeeper	13:34–36
Luke	
Two Debtors	7:41–43
Good Samaritan*	10:30–37
Friend at Midnight	11:5–8
Rich Fool*	12:16–20
Watchful Servants	12:35–38
Barren Fig Tree	13:6–9
Chief Seats	14:7–10
Tower Builder	14:28–30
King at War	14:31–32
Lost Coin	15:8–10
Prodigal Son*	15:11–24
Older Brother*	15:25–32
Dishonest Steward	16:1–8
Rich Man and Lazarus*	16:19–31
Unprofitable Servants	17:7–10
Unjust Judge	18:2–5
Pharisee and Publican*	18:9–14
John	
Good Shepherd	10:1–18
Vine and Branches	15:1–6

I encourage you, the reader, to follow four steps in going through this book:

1. Read the scripture text (given in the chapter head).
2. Read the chapter.
3. Discuss the questions.
4. Read the additional information at the end.

First, I hope you will read the scripture text, indicated in the chapter heading, at least twice. If you read it as a group, out loud, assign speaking parts. Have people do different voices. These are dramatic scenes, but if someone reads the parable quickly in a monotone, you may miss the emotion. Again, I can imagine Jesus using different voices and raising and lowering the decibels as he told the stories. Dramatize them in your group. Discuss how you think a character's voice would have been.

Next you should read the chapter, also twice. Ask yourself how I have understood and applied the parable. Do you agree with my interpretation? Is this interpretation different than what you have heard? Did you expect a different approach? Have you heard sermons or lessons on these parables? How did the preacher or teacher explain them?

Now read the questions at the end of each chapter. These are designed to get you thinking further. You may want to add some questions of your own. At any rate, I hope you are reading this book with others and will discuss these questions. The parables of Jesus are supposed to make you keep thinking. And here's the exciting part of studying the parables, as I noted above: there are many applications. I have only given—and thought of—a few. You will probably think of others.

Finally, the further information that comes after the discussion questions is optional. Read it if you want; forget about it if you want. I'm a teacher; I have to tell these things. If this information enriches your understanding, then I'm glad. If you find after reading some of it that it's a bother, just skip it and move on to the next chapter. I'll try not to cry too much.

DISCUSSION QUESTIONS

1. Are you surprised at how many parables of Jesus are recorded in the four Gospels? What does this say about Jesus's teaching methods?

2. In what sense are the parables Rorschach tests?

3. Do you agree that Jesus may have taken hours to tell some of these parables?

4. What did Jesus mean by his repeated admonition: "Whoever has ears to hear, let him [or her] hear"? How would you paraphrase this plea?

GOING DEEPER

The stories closest to Jesus's own parables are those found in the rabbinic literature. Here is one to illustrate (I'll give more later):

> (Gentiles, women, and uneducated persons cannot be expected to understand the Torah.) They parable a parable. Unto what is the matter like? It is like a king of flesh and blood who told his servant to boil him some broth, though he had never boiled him broth in his life. The result was that he burnt the broth and provoked his master. (t. Beracoth 7:18)[11]

In other words, not everyone is able to interpret the Scriptures. This gift is not for everyone. This statement reminds us of Jesus's words to his disciples:

Matthew 13:10-11	Luke 8:9-10
"And his disciples came to him and said, 'Why do you speak to them in parables?' He answered and said to them, 'Because to you it is given to know the mysteries of the kingdom of heaven, but to them it is not given.'"	"His disciples were asking him what this parable meant. He said, 'To you it is given to know the mysteries of the kingdom of God. But to the rest (the teaching comes) in parables.'"

The difference between the rabbinic parable and Jesus's words is that the rabbis studied for years in order to interpret the Torah responsibly. For Jesus, the key is having his interpretation of the Torah (Old Testament). He was the key, himself. But both texts warn us that a lot of mischief can happen when those unprepared start interpreting the Bible for the rest of the people of God. We all must take Bible interpretation very seriously, lest we "burn the broth." In the coming chapters, I will try not to burn it.

NOTES

[1] See Claus Westermann, *The Parables of Jesus in the Light of the Old Testament* (Minneapolis: Fortress, 1990). For example, 2 Samuel 12:1–7, 14:1–20; Isaiah 5:1–7, 30:13–14; Jeremiah 2:13; Ezekiel 17:2–10; Habakkuk 1:14–16; Psalm 1:2–4.

[2] See Harvey K. McArthur and Robert M. Johnston, *They Also Taught in Parables: Rabbinic Parables from the First Centuries of the Christian Era* (Grand Rapids: Academie, 1990).

[3] B. Brandon Scott, *Hear Then the Parable* (Minneapolis: Fortress, 1990).

[4] M. Connick, *Jesus the Man, the Mission, and the Message* (Edgewood Cliffs, NJ: Prentice Hall, 1974).

[5] Other definitions: "a fictitious saying picturing truth" (Klyne Snodgrass, *Stories with Intent: A Comprehensive Guide to the Parables of Jesus* [Grand Rapids: Eerdmans, 2008]); "a narrative or saying of varying length, designed to illustrate a truth . . ." (Frederick William Danker, *A Greek-English Lexicon of the New Testament and Other Early Christian Literature*, 3rd ed. [Chicago: University of Chicago Press, 2000]).

[6] See David A. Fiensy, *The Message and Ministry of Jesus: An Introductory Textbook* (New York: University Press of America, 1996).

[7] A Danish Christian theologian who lived in the nineteenth century.

[8] Snodgrass, *Stories with Intent.*

[9] Snodgrass, *Stories with Intent.*

[10] The parables with an asterisk* are handled in this book. This table is taken from Fiensy, *The Message and Ministry of Jesus.*

[11] Translation in McArthur and Johnston, *They Also Taught in Parables.*

1

THE SURPRISING GOD

Luke 15:11–24

At one point in our life, my wife and I served in campus ministry in a university in Germany. One of the more important things we did was shepherd Christian believers through sometimes difficult situations. There was one young man who was in his doctoral program and was struggling with a "cranky" professor. This professor, so the student claimed, was mean, impossible to please, and was crushing his spirit. I often met with him for coffee to listen to his complaints and to try to offer solace and advice where possible. The American Thanksgiving holiday was approaching, and we had planned to have as many guests in our tiny apartment as we could. Turkey is not easy to get in Germany, so we had ordered it a month ahead. I walked over to this student's apartment to invite him, his wife, and children to our house the next day (they could not afford a phone). When I arrived, however, I was not greeted with the usual gloom but with happy faces all around. The "cranky" guy had been there already with a turkey and other food for them to cook for American Thanksgiving the next day. That meant that the professor, the "mean guy," had planned at least one month ahead of time to bless this family. The student commented, "I guess this professor is not so mean after all." Ah . . . yeah! How many teachers ever bought you a turkey?

This is the view many people have of the God of Christianity. You can read some nasty stuff about God on Internet websites. They present him as violent, bloodthirsty, cruel, vindictive, petty, and just plain mean. This is a caricature, but it often sticks. After all, if you only read what's on the websites and do not actually read the Bible carefully, no one can blame you for believing this caricature. But this parable from Jesus destroys any false presentation of the God of the Bible. God is not mean-spirited at all but quite surprising. This parable is often named "The Parable of the Prodigal Son." But I want to call it "The Parable of the Surprising God."[1] I think you will see why I want this change.

God is represented, of course, by the father of the story. At three critical turns in the narrative, the father behaves quite surprisingly. These are:

1. The indulgent father
2. The searching father
3. The forgiving father

A man—evidently a very rich man—had a large landed estate and two sons. Now in the Middle East, the older son is the little prince, and all sons after that are mostly spare parts. They are there to replace the older son should he die (see Chapter Twelve). So, it is really presumptuous when the younger son, out of the blue, approaches his father and demands his inheritance. Notice he does not even say "please." He has a sense of entitlement. He is selfish, egocentric, and arrogant. He is really quite a messed-up young man. How old is he? Since fathers usually married off their children rather young in those days (the rabbis suggested the age of eighteen for marrying boys) and there is no mention of a wife, we assume he is in the middle teenage years.[2] So, the kid is around fifteen or sixteen years old and demanding his inheritance. He thinks he knows it all and wants to get out and see the world before he fossilizes into an "aged" eighteen-year-old. That "old man" (father) is holding him back.

Kenneth Bailey[3] spent over forty years teaching the New Testament in various institutions in the Middle East (Lebanon, Jerusalem, Cyprus, and Egypt). He developed the habit of entering Muslim peasant villages and reading them the parables of Jesus and asking them for their reaction. Since they were Muslim and had never heard these stories before, they were a good reaction group for him. Whenever he read this parable, their response was one of horror. What was the younger son saying culturally when he asked for his inheritance like that? What cultural message was there? The villagers almost always responded that the son was wanting the father to die. He was saying, "I want you dead, old man!" The peasants Bailey spoke with were horrified by such a son. He was truly an evil child.

And yet the surprising thing is what the father does. Most Middle Eastern fathers, when approached by such a boy, would have taken a stick and beaten him thoroughly with it. "You want what's coming to you? Here it is!" Whack! Whack! Or, perhaps they would have disinherited him for such brazenness and for such an insult to the honor of the *paterfamilias,* the male head of the household, the family authority in all matters. But this indulgent father gives him what he wants! There is not even a hint of reprimand. He just gives the boy what he wants.

He reminds me of an old movie I saw, *Hondo*, starring John Wayne. In the movie, the star has a mangy dog that follows him around. He comes to a house occupied by a mother and small boy. The boy can't leave the dog alone even though the John Wayne character warns him twice that the dog bites. So, the star lets the matter develop as it will. The boy keeps pestering the dog, and the dog bites the boy. The boy's mother scolds the John Wayne character for allowing this to happen. John Wayne answers, "I told him twice. I figured he had to learn the hard way."

That seems to be the indulgent father's intention in this story. The arrogant boy must learn the hard way. Some people just will not listen to counsel. God has told us the way we should go more than twice, but people just keep "pestering the dog."

This is the lesson the apostle Paul gives us in Romans 1:24, 26, and 28. He lists the sins of the pagans all the way from idolatry to ruthlessness. Three times in this long list of vices Paul writes, "God gave them over to their sinful desires . . ." In other words, with God you get what you want. God forces no one to live according to his moral principles. He forces no one to develop a relationship with him. He compels no one to spend eternity with him.

Further, God is not eagerly waiting to zap everyone with a lightning bolt every time they sin. We zap ourselves. We keep pestering the dog until it bites us. We create a world of greed and selfishness and then whine when someone takes advantage of us or defrauds us. We engage in sexual behavior outside of our marriage and then feel let down when our relationship collapses, we contract an STD, or we end up alone. We become fascinated with violence and the power it gives us and then respond angrily when there is yet another mass shooting somewhere. God does not zap us; we zap ourselves. God gives us over to our sinful desires until the dog bites.

So, the first surprising turn of this story is the fact that the *father gives this brat exactly what he wants.* With God you get what you want—or what you *think* you want.

The second surprise is that the father never gives up on the boy. So, the kid goes to a "far country" to spend his loot. The Jewish hearers of the story probably would have pictured a pagan city, something like Gerasa, east of the Jordan River. The money (silver coins) is burning a hole in his pocket. He probably spends his money on drink and gambling, evidently paying for his newly acquired friends to enjoy themselves as well. We also find out later in the parable (verse 30) that he spent a lot of it on prostitutes.

Then, suddenly, the fortune is gone. How can you burn through a fortune in such a short time? It's like those people that win the lottery and take home tens of millions of dollars. Often within two years they are completely broke. How could they spend that much money in such a short time? I have never understood it, but they do. So it was with this young man. When you have a lot, you think it will never end. But it does. And then, the friends are gone. They were not really friends anyway. Shortly after his financial exhaustion, a famine arises and the price of food skyrockets. The only job he can find is feeding pigs. Clearly, he is in a gentile area. He is so hungry that the pig food (carob pods) starts to look good to him. When pig food appeals to your tastes, it is probably time for a life adjustment.

So, what is the father doing? Since, when the son finally returns home, the father sees him a long distance away, we must presume that the father was regularly out on the hillside searching the horizon for his boy. This is the second surprising fact about God. Although he *gives* you what you think you want, he never *gives up* on you.

People often report their feeling that God pursued them. It reminds me of the testimony of C. S. Lewis. Lewis comments in his autobiographical work that he never pursued God but always felt that God was pursuing him. He says that God was the hunter and he was the deer. God targeted him, took aim, fired, and hit his target. He felt that God was unrelenting in his pursuit.

Does God pursue people? Yes, that is the point. He does not force you—you get what you want—but he pursues you. Just as the father in the parable kept searching the horizon for any sign of his son, God searches our lives for any sign that we want to "come home." The second surprise of this parable is that *the father never gave up on the arrogant boy,* no matter how unworthy he may have been.

The third surprise is that the father forgives. So, the kid has a flash of insight. He is evidently living in squalor or perhaps sleeping on the streets. He eats almost nothing. He is filthy and cold. Those "friends" won't look at him, let alone loan him money. The ladies he had been paying for their favors are no longer paying him any mind. He is alone, poor, and miserable. Only then does he realize what a jerk he has been.

The kid seems to have genuine repentance. He thinks to himself, "I'll go back and tell my father, 'Father, I have sinned against God and you. I'm a jerk, an idiot, an arrogant and undeserving child. I know you don't want me back as a son, but I'm begging you, just give me a job. I'll work for minimum wage. I just want to be near you and my home.'"

Well, he didn't use those exact words, but that's what his words meant. So, the once proud, selfish, entitled brat has become humble, submissive, and repentant. That's what we call saving faith. Don't say to God, "I'll become a Christian but don't expect me to serve in some way, to give any of my money to others, or even to attend church regularly." Be like the younger son. Humble yourself and ask God to give you a minimum-wage job.

So, the father is out at his regularly appointed time to scan the horizon, and he sees this beaten-down, dirty, sickly looking person coming toward him. That can't be his son. His son was healthy and hardy the last time he saw him. He left with expensive clothing and with his arrogant little head held high. This guy can't be him.

But there is something about that walk . . . It *is* his son! Oh my! That beaten-down sample of humanity is his boy! The father runs to the boy and embraces him immediately. Even though the son is filthy and smelly, the father wraps his arms around him. The boy is probably sick with some sort of terrible disease as a result of living in squalor for weeks or months, but the father pays no attention to that. Nothing else matters except that his son is back.

And here, in verse 20, we have an unusual Greek word: *splagchnizomai*. Try saying that quickly three times. It was used to describe a strong emotional response, a response of great, great compassion (see "Going Deeper" below). Jesus uses it frequently in his teaching. It will pop up a few more times in the parables that follow in this book (Matt. 18:27 in Chapter Four and Luke 10:33 in Chapter Eleven). The word is often used at a turning point in the narrative. At any rate, it denotes here the father's strong compassion and pity for his son. The son asks for the meagerest sort of pity; the father responds with overwhelming compassion. The father's worst nightmare about his son has almost happened. But he is home now. What relief! What joy!

The son starts to give his well-rehearsed speech ("Father, I have sinned—"), but the father cuts him off. He orders his servants to put a really nice robe on the shivering body, to bring sandals for the sore feet, to place a ring on the bony finger. He kisses his smelly, dirty son and orders a banquet. "Kill the stall-fed calf" (the delicacy saved for very special occasions). He declares, "My son was lost and is found; he was dead and is alive!" You can't imagine more drama than that. Try to imagine the father's relief and joy. (He must often have thought, "Is my son dead?")

The son has come home. But he only came to his senses after his experience of hardship. He only realized his behavior when he suffered. It often takes hardship for us to come to our senses. The great hymn writer and preacher John Newton was a slaver who cared nothing for the humanity and suffering of the Africans he transported across the ocean—until he was shipwrecked and nearly drowned. After that, he began to see his life for what it was: a piece of garbage. He converted and ultimately wrote the great hymn, "Amazing Grace."

A more recent example is the story of Andrew Palau. Andrew is the son of the famous preacher Luis Palau of Argentina. Luis is an internationally known evangelist, perhaps more famous outside North America than he is to most Americans. Andrew was a "prodigal son" in the worst way. By his own account, he lived a life of sin, engaging in drugs and immoral sexual activity. His life was spiraling downward and he contemplated suicide. Then his famous father, who never gave up on him, urged him to a summer camp in Jamaica. There he met Christian young people his age and began to reconsider his life. In the end, he came home and is now an evangelist in his own right.[4]

But notice what the father did not do. First, he did not reject the son. By rights he should have. I'm sure the others in the nearby village were scandalized when the father accepted his son. The son had shamed the father and the entire family—for that matter, the entire village—and should have been cut loose for life, perhaps even killed by the village. But the father just forgave the boy.

Nor does the father make the boy beg. The boy can't even get his speech out entirely. The father embraced him immediately. The father does not say, "Well, I might forgive you if you work for me and do a good job for about five years. If you prove yourself first, then I might forgive you." The father just forgives. He is so relieved and so full of joy that his wayward child has returned! All he can think about is his joy.

That is the third surprising thing about this story. *The Father just forgives.* The boy does nothing to deserve forgiveness. It is not that the boy is so great or good that he earns forgiveness. The point is that the father is so kind and loving that he can't help himself. He is by nature forgiving.

God just forgives. Never mind that it often takes misfortune, a setback, an illness, or some sort of loss to cause us to cast aside our greed, arrogance, and self-centeredness. He still forgives. *No matter what you have done, where you have been, what you have seen, God will forgive you if you repent.*

I became a Christian at the age of nine. It happened after a special speaker appeared at our church. He was an old man. (Or so he appeared to me. When you're nine, every adult looks old.) He told about an experience in his teen years. At the age of sixteen, he quarreled bitterly with his father. He wanted to become a movie star. He may have had the looks, since as an older man, he seemed rather striking. His father, a farmer from Illinois, thought that was the craziest idea he had ever heard. Even if the boy could do that—unlikely—why would anyone want to do it? So, the son and father had harsh words. That night the boy slipped out of the house and ran away. He hopped a freight train as it passed by his house and rode it all the way to California. There he lived for over a year trying to get his big break. He became involved in many sinful practices. At the end of this time, he was living in poverty and his health was nearly ruined by his lifestyle. He decided it was time to go home. He did not know if his father would have him back, however. So, he called collect (before cell phones) and got his mother. She begged him to return. He said, "Let me talk to Dad." He was sure his father would be angry with him for leaving as he did and for living as he had. He was sure his dad would have many questions, such as, "What have you been doing? What sinful practices have you indulged in? How have you shamed the family?" But his dad got on the phone and just said, "Son, come home. Just come home." That illustration of God's love convinced me to become a Christian.

That's what this story is saying to all of us. *Just come home.*

I've wandered far away from God,
    Now I'm coming home;
The paths of sin too long I've trod,
    Lord, I'm coming home.

Coming home, coming home,
    Nevermore to roam;
Open wide Thine arms of love;
    Lord, I'm coming home.[5]

So, this parable is telling us that God, like this forgiving father, awaits us all. He just wants us to come home. No matter what you have done, where you have been, what you have seen, God will forgive you if you repent.

DISCUSSION QUESTIONS

1. Why do you think God lets us have what we want? Shouldn't he stop us?

2. Since the father in the parable forgave the son so readily, does that seem to underplay reforming your life? Does God just forgive us so easily every time?

3. When have you felt like God was pursuing you?

4. What "far countries" do people run to today?

GOING DEEPER

Kenneth Bailey traveled from Morocco to India and from Turkey to Sudan to ask villagers what they thought about the younger son in the parable of the prodigal son. Every time, the villagers responded something like this:

> "Has anyone ever made such a request in your village?"
>
> (That is, for the father to give inheritance before he dies.)
>
> "Never!"
>
> "Could anyone ever make such a request?"
>
> "Impossible!"
>
> "If anyone ever did, what would happen?"
>
> "His father would beat him, of course!"
>
> "Why?"
>
> "This request means—he wants his father to die!"[6]

When the younger son sold his share of the estate to take the money and spend it, he contravened custom. They simply did not ever sell their land. It was almost like a part of their family. To them, land was not a commodity but a sacred trust.[7] The boy has no respect for the land.

Evidently, a son's running away from home, falling into hard times, and begging to come home happened frequently in the ancient world. Here is a part of an actual letter written from a young man to his mother asking to be forgiven and taken back: "Antonius Longus to Nilous his mother . . . I was ashamed to come to Karanis because I go about in filth. I wrote to you that I am naked. I beg you, mother, be reconciled to me. Well, I know what I have brought on myself. I have received a fitting lesson. I know that I have sinned . . ." (A. S. Hunt and C. C. Edgar, *Select Papyri,* LCL).[8]

And here is a rabbinic parable featuring another runaway: "A king had a son who had gone astray from his father a journey of a hundred days; his friends said to him, 'Return to your father;' he said, 'I cannot.' Then his father sent to say, 'Return as far as you can, and I will come to you the rest of the way.' So God says, 'Return to me, and I will return to you.'"[9]

When the father runs to the son, he does a very undignified and almost shameful thing. Grown men do not run, especially not to their adult sons. When he orders a banquet with a slaughtered animal to eat, he pays the son a great compliment. This was only done for very honored guests. The shamed and shaming son returns from his sinful and hurtful (to the family) past, and the father . . . throws him a huge party!

No doubt, when Jesus told this story in Galilean villages, many shouted "No!" when he said the father embraced the son. The culture expected the father to beat the kid, maybe even kill him. The father's forgiveness is rather scandalous. Should we imagine that some village men rose from their places upon hearing this ending and stormed away out of disgust? No man of honor would receive a wayward son like that!

Getting back to that word for compassion in verse 20, the Greek word *splagchnizomai,* it is taken from the word meaning the "intestines" or "inner organs." Since the Greeks thought the emotions came from the abdominal organs, they used the word for these parts metaphorically to mean strong emotion, especially strong compassion. In most cases in the New Testament, the word is only used of God's compassion, as in this parable. But in the Parable of the Good Samaritan (Luke 10:30–35), it is used for the Samaritan.[10] Watch for this striking term in two parables that follow in this book.

NOTES

[1] Robert Capon, *Kingdom, Grace, Judgment: Paradox, Outrage, and Vindication in the Parables of Jesus* (Grand Rapids: Eerdmans, 2002), notes in several places in his book that the parables have been misnamed. This parable is really about the father, not the two sons. The two sons help show what the father is like.

[2] On the average age at marriage and the marriage process, see David A. Fiensy, *The Archaeology of Daily Life: Ordinary Persons in the Late Second Temple Israel* (Eugene, OR: Cascade, 2020).

[3] See Kenneth Bailey, *Poet and Peasant and through Peasant Eyes: A Literary-Cultural Approach to the Parables in Luke* (Grand Rapids: Eerdmans, 1983).

[4] See his story in Lee Strobel, *The Case for Grace* (Grand Rapids: Zondervan, 2015).

[5] Words by William J. Kirkpatrick (1892).

[6] Bailey, *Poet and Peasant and through Peasant Eyes.*

[7] See David A. Fiensy, *The Social History of Palestine in the Herodian Period: The Land Is Mine* (Lewiston: Edwin Mellen, 1991).

[8] Quoted in Fiensy, *Message and Ministry of Jesus.*

[9] Pesikta Rabbati 184b. Translation in C. G. Montefiore and H. Loewe, *A Rabbinic Anthology* (New York: Shocken, 1974).

[10] See Helmut Köster, "*splagchnizomai,*" in G. Kittel, ed., *Theological Dictionary of the New Testament* (Grand Rapids: Eerdmans, 1964–1976), 7.548–59.

2

BUSY, BUSY, BUSY

Luke 14:15–24

There is a funny commercial going around now—advertising some brand of beef jerky—that has a group of campers meeting up with the legendary Sasquatch or Bigfoot. Do they take photos to prove that the creature really exists? No. Do they call in the press to cover the sensational story? No. What do they do? They play a prank on him! Seriously? The most sensational wildlife discovery of the century and all those knuckleheads can think to do is play a practical joke on this creature. I think they have missed the point.

This parable is about persons who miss the point. You only get one life. Don't blow it. Don't miss the point. In the parable there are three types of persons: the Benevolent, the Busy, and the Bruised. The Benevolent person, the person hosting a banquet, is, of course, God. The banquet represents the kingdom of God. Notice two things here:

First, the Benevolent man (God) is just a wealthy person who has great resources and who wants to do something nice for the people of his village. He has cooked up a great amount of food, perhaps decorated a banquet hall, asked storytellers and musicians to prepare some entertainment, and then invited his guests. We should probably think that the guests had previous notice that there would be a banquet on such and such a night. They knew it was coming. The rich man just wants to bless his village.

Second, notice that he invites the guests to a banquet. The banquet is a good metaphor for the kingdom of God. Banquets were events of rejoicing, good food, and fellowship. They were times of joy and celebration. This is what the kingdom of God is supposed to be: a celebration of the great God who created us and redeemed us, and fellowship with people of faith. It is a deception to represent the church as a fun-spoiling institution. The church—at its best—brings out the true joys of life and enhances the great pleasures of life: fellowship, family, and faith.

Most of us who have grown up in America or Western Europe have believed the big lie. If we can get rich and accumulate things, we will be happy, we think. If that were true, Americans should be the happiest people on the planet. Instead, we worry about nuclear war with North Korea, mass shootings in schools and churches, suicide rates, sexual abuse, and opioid addiction, among other things. I don't think it's working.

But this definition of the kingdom is also a lesson and an admonition to us. Is your church a celebration or a lamentation? Do people leave your church services feeling uplifted or abused? Do those who associate with your people feel valued or judged? We need to restore the sense of joy in being a Christian and restore the affirmation for others, even those struggling with sin, addiction, and bad behavior. We help, we counsel, and we admonish/confront with love. Only God is fit to judge.

Joy is the echo of God's life within us. Let's be sure to echo who God is, not who we have become from living through church squabbles and enduring judgmental fellow Christians. Project who God is and what God is offering each of us.

So, the Benevolent one gets everything ready and then sends his servants out into the streets to issue the final invitation: "It's all ready. Come to the feast."

But then the invitees respond with shameful ingratitude and rudeness. There are three rejections named in the parable: First a guy says he has just bought a field and has to go see it. "Sorry, can't come to your wonderful gesture of generosity and friendship. I have business." Really? He couldn't wait until the next day to see his field? He had to insult the Benevolent one like this? We are suspicious of such an excuse. The excuse in itself might be reasonable, but the timing is not. Who would buy a field without looking at it first? It was a great insult to refuse someone's hospitality in the ancient Near East.

The second guy says he has bought ten oxen and has to go try them out. He is like a farmer who has just purchased a new tractor or a new combine. "Sorry, Rich Guy, I have just bought this new John Deere tractor and I have to get on it right now and ride it up and down the rows of corn. I want to see how fast it can go and work all the controls. Playing with my new tractor is much more important than being polite and appreciative of your kind invitation to enjoy good food, good fellowship, and friendship. Your feelings don't really matter to me as much as my feelings of giddiness at having a new toy." Again, he didn't examine the oxen first? I expect he did. This is just an excuse. Shameful.

The third guy says he has just gotten married and must go home. Seriously? He just got married this minute? I don't think so. I think we should envision someone who has married within the last few weeks. He couldn't come to the banquet for at least a little while and so honor the Benevolent one? This again looks more like an excuse to save face.

Now there is nothing wrong with people who give their all in their job or profession. And certainly Christians should be all about strengthening and preserving their marriages. These are things God wants you to do. They are very good things. Paul writes in Colossians 3:17 that everything we do we should do "in the name of the Lord Jesus," as if we were doing it for God (compare 1 Cor. 10:31). That means that the carpenter, the gas station attendant, the stockbroker, the banker, the teacher, and so forth should see their work as if they're doing it for God. So, do your very best. Be honest. Strive to succeed. To want to succeed and climb the ladder in your chosen field is a good thing. But don't do these things to the neglect of God. These are, on paper, reasonable excuses, but their timing is suspect. You can always find a justification for stiffing God out of his time with you. Are you sure it is an appropriate justification?

I knew a man who was a vice president in a large corporation. He was also an active member of the church my wife and I attended. He began saying that his life's goal was to be a millionaire by the time he turned forty. He began volunteering for more weekend work to rise further in his job. He missed church more and more. Finally, he never came to church at all. When I would talk with him, I could tell that his zeal for God had cooled considerably. He had started worshipping money and success.

Be successful if you can, but never at the expense of your faith. Hard work has its place; hard work is good for us. But doing anything to the neglect of God is not.

Keep your marriage strong as well. Take time for your spouse. Go on dates. Take trips together, just the two of you. Communicate your feelings and admiration for your spouse regularly. A strong marriage is one of the greatest blessings of life. Don't blow it by neglect. But never put your spouse ahead of God. That is one way to blow it.

These people have forgotten about the quickness of life. James writes, "For what is your life? It is a mist that is here for a little while and then disappears" (James 4:14). Life goes so quickly that we can, before we know it—by bad habits and neglect—find ourselves having given ourselves to obsessions, addictions, vanity, narcissism, and self-serving pleasure. Then, one day we wake up and ask, "What has it all been for?" You only get one life. Don't blow it. Don't forget to ask yourself regularly, "What is my purpose in life? What is my calling?"

A really good movie, *Hereafter,* was released some years back. In this movie, three individuals had had an experience—a near-death experience or some contact with a dead person—that made them think about the afterlife. Now I don't know if we have contact with dead people, but the lesson of the movie is still a good one. These three people had been busy going about their ordinary, worldly lives. They had had no time for spiritual interests. But these new experiences had forced them to think about eternity. In one scene a lady laments having to think about spiritual things. She longs for her old life back, when she could be shallow and worldly. It seems odd that someone who has been raised to a higher spiritual plane would long for shallowness and emptiness. I think the oddness was the point. Most of us prefer the easy route in which we do not have to think about spiritual matters. We would rather be self-absorbed. We can just have our comfortable lifestyle, our entertainment, our sports, and our pleasures, and forget about serious issues. Oh, for the good old days when we only thought about the latest fashions or music!

I remember a few years ago asking a graduating high school senior what his plans were. Usually they talk about college or a job or the military. But his response was: "I have tickets to the Who concert." Okay. We can excuse such shallowness in an eighteen-year-old. But what's your excuse? That's it? That's your life?

All of these things remind me of a story about a man whose house caught fire. His security system reported the fire to the fire department. The fire trucks came and were putting out the fire. All of this was unknown to the owner of the house, who was in his basement playing video games with his earphones on. He was so involved in the game, so obsessed with succeeding in his make-believe world, so absorbed by his activity, that he did not notice a fire above him! What a perfect metaphor for most people living in comfort and luxury in the Western Hemisphere. We are so absorbed in our pleasures that we don't know our house is on fire.

A preacher told a true story in a sermon I heard once. He had this young guy in his church who bought a hardware store. This guy was very ambitious and hardworking. Early on he began to start skipping church events. He opened the store at 9:00 A.M. each day, except Sundays, when he opened it at 1:00 P.M. He closed it most days at 8:00 P.M. He was always busy either working at the store, preparing to open the store, or restocking the store. The years passed, and the preacher saw less and less of the hardware store owner. He aged, and his spiritual life went to the dogs. His wife and kids came to church, but he had clearly given it up entirely. His store was everything to him. Whenever the preacher would encounter him and gently invite him to a service, he always got the same answer, "I can't close the store." Well, the man did not live a long life. He died in his late forties. The preacher did his funeral, and climbed into the funeral coach to make the trip to the cemetery. On the way to the cemetery, they passed the hardware store. There was a large sign hanging in the window: "CLOSED TODAY." God had closed his store. God will close every store someday. You only get one life. Don't blow it.

I love the words of David Watson: "Make Christ first over all that you own. We must hold everything with an open palm (our ambitions, our possessions). Christ can take away whatever he wants and add whatever he wants."

Mother Teresa said: "Make sure you let God's grace work in your souls by accepting whatever he gives you and giving him whatever he takes from you." Yes, that is the point.

The Benevolent, the Busy, and now the Bruised. So, the Benevolent man was insulted by their refusal of his kind invitation, and he ordered his servants to go out in the streets and alleys—and then the country roads—and bring in the sick, the smelly, and the filthy. These are the persons whom life has kicked around. They are not notable people; they are not attractive people; they do not belong to any country club. They are the desperately poor. They are the outcasts of society, the dregs of humanity. They are doubtless homeless, sleeping in the streets and alleys. They are hungry. The invitation to a banquet to eat all they could hold must seem like heaven to them. They are dirty, stinky, sickly—they probably coughed wretchedly throughout the banquet—and many probably have a severe disability, either mental or physical. These would have been a seedy, ugly group invited to a lavish banquet prepared for the snobbish rich.

There are so many Bruised people out there. I was in college when I was somehow invited to preach at a homeless shelter one evening. They would admit the homeless around 6:00 P.M., give them dinner, a mandatory sermon, then a bed for the night. It was wintertime and cold outside. I come from a small midwestern town where, if we had homeless, I never saw them. I grew up under the idea that if someone was homeless, it was probably his or her fault. "Go get a job if you are homeless," we would have said. So, I was unprepared for what I saw that night.

They let them in on time, and they walked quickly to the dinner table. They were allowed a sandwich and a bowl of soup. Most stuffed an entire sandwich into their mouth while in the line and put another one on their plate as well. After dinner, as they walked upstairs for the sermon, I noticed that many grabbed another sandwich and crammed it into their jaws. Upstairs as I rose to preach, after a bit of singing, I was stunned by the look of desperation on their faces. I had never seen, in person, people so desperate, hopeless, and sad. I just threw out the sermon I had written and talked to them—ad lib—about how much God loved each of them. The Bruised.

I read an inspiring story in Lee Strobel's little book *The Case for Grace*. Stephanie Fast was born in Korea to a Korean mother and an American father. She never knew her father at all. In Korean society, to have such a child in the family was a great shame. She was both illegitimate and of mixed race. These are double humiliations in Korea. So, at age four, her extended family told her mother that she had to get rid of the child. The mother put Stephanie on a train and told her to ride it until it stopped. There she would get off and an uncle would meet her. She did as she was told—imagine sending a four-year-old child on such a long journey—but there was, of course, no uncle at the end of the ride. She was on her own. She lived for the next three years on the streets. She ate mice and insects to stay alive. At age seven, an orphanage took her in as a sort of working child. She was not really up for adoption but was allowed to stay if she worked. But one day an American missionary couple came to adopt a baby and noticed the filthy, lice-infected girl. They decided to take her. She grew up in America and is today a Christian inspirational writer and speaker. The Bruised.

Well, we are all in that category, aren't we? Until we realize and accept it, we cannot appreciate grace. We can deny our state—playing video games in our basement—but it does not change the state. We are Bruised and in need of the banquet. How we need the generosity of the Benevolent one. How we need the fellowship of our fellow banqueters. How we need the nourishment of that banquet.

Charlotte Elliott lived in nineteenth-century England. She had grown up in the church but was always fearful that she was not good enough for God. Then, at age thirty-two, she suffered a debilitating illness that left her suffering for the next fifty years. One day, a Swiss pastor visited her and asked if she was right with God. She was angry at the question and responded rudely. She later summoned him to her to apologize and say that she wanted to clean up her life first before getting right with God. The Swiss pastor responded, "Come just as you are." She gave her life to Christ that day. Years later she remembered those words, and they inspired her to write her famous hymn:

> Just as I am, without one plea, but that thy blood was
> shed for me.
> And that thou bidd'st me come to thee, O Lamb of God,
> I come.
> Just as I am, poor, wretched, blind; sight, riches, healing
> of the mind,
> Yea, all I need, in thee to find, O Lamb of God, I come.

Whether you are busy or bruised as you read this, I hope you will accept the kindness and grace of the Benevolent One. Think about your life—its brevity, and its seriousness. Come to the feast.

DISCUSSION QUESTIONS

1. Do you think most churches today live in celebration or in lamentation? Do they really believe the kingdom of God is a

banquet, or do they act like it is distasteful medicine that you just have to put up with?

2. How can we as Christians help those immersed in materialism to see that they need to think about their spiritual life?

3. Did you grow up in the church? If so, did you ever have a time in which you drifted away due to the busyness of life? If not, how did you become (or stay) interested in leading a spiritual life?

4. Do you agree that all of us are bruised in some way?

GOING DEEPER

The cultural signals in this parable were evident to the Jewish listeners but are not to us. The excuses for not attending the banquet are just the Middle Eastern way of saying, "No, I don't want to attend your stupid banquet. I consider you below my status in society." The first one invited, according to Bruce Malina and Richard Rohrbaugh,[1] was probably a large absentee landowner living in a city (where this story probably takes place). The second has bought enough oxen to plow 110 acres of land. That is quite a large farm in this part of the world at that time.[2] These are rich and snobbish persons.

Again, Kenneth Bailey's experience teaching the New Testament in the Middle East for forty years can help us. If someone is invited to attend a dinner in the Middle East and cannot attend, he is expected to offer a plausible excuse. If he does not offer a believable excuse, it is a clear insult. None of these excuses are reasonable. In the first place, Bailey notes, no one would buy a field without looking at it. Too many fields are rocky and barren. That would be lunacy in the Middle East. The second invitee also offers an unlikely excuse. No one would even bid on a pair of oxen, let alone buy them, without inspecting them very carefully. They have to be well matched in strength and stamina or they cannot plow together. The last excuse (he has taken a wife) is not only lame but even pornographic. It's like saying, "I have a woman in the back of the house, and I am busy with her." All of these excuses are an insult to the banquet host. They have left him no room to save face. He is completely dishonored by their shameless and insulting behavior.[3] This is how Jesus's Middle Eastern audience would have heard his parable.

There is an interesting rabbinic story that is parallel to this one. A rich tax collector, Bar Mayan, was despised by the community (compare Chapter Six). He wanted to ingratiate himself to his village. So, he tried to give a huge banquet and invite the village elders in order to be accepted in society. Giving them a banquet would, he hoped, change their minds about him. But, alas, the invited guests did not come. They stated clearly that they wanted nothing to do with Bar Mayan. So, he invited the poor to come so the food would not go to waste.[4] Evidently, when food was left over from these banquets, they often gave it to the poor (unlike in the case of Lazarus; see Chapter Ten). The story Jesus tells, then, might have happened numerous times in Palestine before and during his ministry. But this all highlights the fact that the excuses are just a way of saying, "I don't want your banquet or you. Leave me alone!"

The parallel text to this one in Luke is in Matthew 22:1–14. In this version of the Banquet Parable, the dinner is being given for the wedding of the king's son. The excuses of the reluctant invitees are also a bit different. Further, Matthew has an additional bit about a guy coming to the banquet improperly dressed. Why do you think there are those differences? Shouldn't the texts in the two Gospels read identically? Shouldn't they be photocopies of one another? What happened? Do you think Jesus told this parable only once, or did he tell it many times, adapting it to the village culture in which he found himself each evening? And what about Matthew's and Luke's church communities? Did they retell these parables?

NOTES

[1] Bruce J. Malina and Richard L. Rohrbaugh, *Social-Science Commentary on the Synoptic Gospels* (Minneapolis: Fortress, 1992).

[2] See Fiensy, *Social History of Palestine in the Herodian Period.*

[3] Kenneth Bailey, *Jesus through Middle Eastern Eyes* (Downers Grove, IL: InterVarsity Press, 2008).

[4] Joachim Jeremias, *The Parables of Jesus* (New York: Charles Scribner's Sons, 1963). See also the same story with a further development in Chapter Ten.

3

GOD IS NOT FAIR!

Matt. 20:1–16

I can still see the white orb flying through the air toward Mr. M—'s head. I was in the eleventh grade. We had just come inside from a snowy day and a kid had brought a snowball with him. He sat down next to me, put the snowball on my desk, and said, "I dare you to throw this toward the blackboard up front." So, I'm fifteen years old and I think, "Sure. Why not?" That's why fifteen-year-olds should not drive a car. Without looking or thinking, I picked up the snowball and threw it as hard as I could toward the blackboard. Then I saw the teacher, Mr. M—, standing right in the line of fire. He turned to face me just as the snowball whizzed by his head and smacked up against the board. "Who threw that?" he yelled. I stood to confess. "Get to the principal's office now!" I went to the office wondering if I might go to prison and do hard time, maybe work on the rock pile for a few years, maybe have to break out in a daring escape by tunneling under walls or crawling through sewers or something. I had my next twenty years all planned out, and they didn't look good. The principal, however, was more amused than anything about the whole deal. He advised me to go back and apologize for the incident and let the teacher assign punishment. Now this teacher was notoriously rough. I once saw him whack a kid in the mouth with a clipboard because he talked too much. Another time, he ran down the "wild kid," got him in the classic full nelson wrestling hold, and carried him to the office all while the overgrown, out-of-his-mind teenager kicked his shins and punched at him. He taught both American History and some of the Physical Education classes. He was always making guys do push-ups or laps for misbehaving. So, I thought, "Whew, I guess prison's off the table. But maybe I'll have to run a couple of marathons to make up for this." But when I approached Mr. M— and explained what happened, he seemed very understanding. He said my apology was enough and that we would just forget about it. Generous forgiveness. That was a great day.

This parable is about generous forgiveness. God is so generous that sometimes people complain about it. "God is not fair!" some people whine. "That person shouldn't be forgiven. That person shouldn't have a chance to go to heaven." God is unfair.

In the parable Jesus says, "Yes, you are correct. God is unfair. He grades on the curve. He forgives when nobody else in the universe would." In the parable, the workers that worked more than one hour complained that the estate owner (God) rewarded the one-hour worker the same as them. The estate owner was unfairly generous. The estate owner replied: "It's my money. I can do with it as I want." It's God's grace. He can offer it to whom he wants.

Such grace is quite strange to the world. Many years ago, a rock group called *Genesis* sang a song called "No Son of Mine." In the song, the son leaves home under a cloud. Many years later, he wants to reconcile with his father (hmm . . . reminds me of Chapter One). The father replies to the son's overtures, "No, you're no son of mine." The boy had rejected the father years before; now, the father would reject the son. That is exactly the opposite of God's generous forgiveness.

I remember seeing an interview on television many years ago with the famous atheist Madalyn Murray O'Hair. This interview took place shortly after her son, William Murray, had converted to Christianity. She, of course, denounced him and cut him off from the family. Someone in the audience where the interview was conducted asked her if she would forgive and accept her son, should he renounce his newly found faith and come back to her. I'll never forget her answer: "No. Forgiveness is a Christian idea, not mine." Generous forgiveness is not the way of the world.

Generous forgiveness does not judge. The all-day workers in the parable felt it was unfair to be placed in the same category as the one-hour workers. Many of us think we have served Christ for a number of years and we deserve a kind of bonus. We should get bonus points for our years of service. It does not seem fair that people can more or less waltz in at the last minute, repent, and be saved. They shouldn't be given the same benefits as we who have served so long. Or perhaps some think certain sins or certain sinful lifestyles should not be forgiven—ever.

Jeffrey Dahmer was a serial murderer. He murdered seventeen persons from 1978 to 1991. He was sentenced to sixteen life sentences in 1991. He was killed in prison a few months after his sentence. But before he died, news came of his conversion to Christianity. He had accepted Christ in a chapel service and had been baptized in the prison whirlpool. I'll never forget the response that many Christians had that next Sunday when I reported to them the news of his conversion. Many were skeptical; others refused to believe that God could forgive such evil. One guy said,

"If Jeffrey Dahmer is going to be in heaven, I don't want to go there." As I say, God forgives people that nobody else in the universe will.

But God sees many things that we do not. That sinner who recently has repented may be closer to God than many of us who have been Christians for fifty years. Maybe his helplessness has opened him to a deeper understanding of God's grace. We are quick to judge other people's situations, forgetting that only God is qualified to do so. He sees the heart. And when God says, "Forgiven," the forgiveness is total. All of us are undeserving. So, none of us can judge.

In the late 1970s, the Khmer Rouge under the dictator Pol Pot took over Cambodia. During his reign of terror, two million people, out of a population of eight million, were killed in one of the worse genocides in history. He established a system of prison camps for those who opposed him. One of these prison camps, called S-21, was commanded by the notorious and sinister Comrade Duch. During his command of this prison, fourteen thousand persons died through torture and starvation. Only seven prisoners survived the camp. He was a vicious, brutal psychopath. After the Khmer Rouge were driven out by the Vietnamese, Comrade Duch disappeared. One of those who had suffered but survived this genocide, LaPel, was a Christian, and he began conducting evangelistic crusades in the newly liberated country.

Fast-forward to 1994, and LaPel was conducting such a crusade in a Cambodian village. One of those present at the preaching, sitting in the back, kept looking toward the floor. He said nothing but came to every meeting. Finally, he came forward to the altar call and said he wanted to become a Christian. He said his name was Hang Pin. After that, Hang Pin turned into a dynamo. He went to his home village and led several to Christ. He began to travel around Cambodia to share the gospel like other evangelists. He also worked with World Vision. Then, in 1999, someone from the press discovered that the dynamic new Christian called Hang Pin was none other than the formerly nefarious Comrade Duch. After questioning, he admitted his past. He was tried and sentenced to life in prison. There he continues to minister as a Christian to those in prison. What is even more striking is that of the fourteen thousand people Hang Pin/Comrade Duch murdered in prison, one of them was the cousin of LaPel, the man who converted and baptized Hang Pin.[1] Will Comrade Duch be in heaven? Will he also receive "one denarius?" Of course. If you don't believe that, you don't know the "unfair" God, the generous God, the God of enormous grace.

Generous forgiveness is also contagious. Don't worry about whether you've worked all day or only a little while. Be like those paymasters in the parable who, at the end of the day, dispensed the same one denarius pay to everyone. The landowner gave of his generosity, but the paymasters got to actually give out the pay. Imagine how much they enjoyed seeing the look of surprised joy on the faces of the one-hour workers. In the work of the gospel, God is the landowner but we are the paymasters. Be the kind of worker that brings joy into people's lives.

Susie and her two small children were homeless. A Christian couple had seen her and her little ones sleeping under bridges and walking the streets, and they wanted to help. They went to a social agency and told them about Susie. The agency helped Susie find a place for her and the kids to live and helped her find a job. Others in the church contributed food and clothing. Susie became a Christian not long after that. One year after meeting the Christian couple, Susie stood up in church to give her testimony. She was now sober; she had a job; she believed that she could now be a good mother. She had been confused before. She had been lost, but now she was found. Now she had joy, love, direction, and life. She had "come home." She was saved. Fast-forward to today.

Susie now teaches a Sunday school class. She maintains, "If you know anyone who doubts Jesus is alive, let them talk to me."

We try to comprehend the generous God even though we are weak and often fall into judging peoples' lives and behavior. We may at times even hope, secretly, that God never offers some persons "one denarius." But then, we hear about how a Christian's reflection of God's mercy has affected a lost soul.

A homeless drug addict and former prison inmate was living in the city park of Las Vegas. His life, his obsession—his god, really—was heroin. I wonder if I had known him at this time how I would have regarded him. Would I have reflected that he had probably grown up in an abusive home (he did)? Would I have concluded that he had probably run away from home at an early age (age thirteen)? Would I have sympathized with him because his only comfort in life had become drugs?

After he ran away from home, our homeless man lived in a commune for a while, until he committed a crime and was sentenced to juvenile prison for a year. There he became a hardened and skilled criminal. Once out of prison, his life led to more serious crimes (drug trafficking) and heroin addiction. He served two more stints in prison (a total of eight years). Ultimately, his heroin habit destroyed everything in his life. He was left homeless, dirty, hungry, and irretrievably addicted. He reached a level in which he was so dirty that even the other homeless guys couldn't stand to be around him. They all told him, "Find somewhere to take a shower!"

That's when he heard about a church in the Las Vegas area that offered free showers and clean clothes to homeless people. So, he went there to take a shower, and something happened that changed everything. Sometimes a moment of generosity—in imitation of the generous God—can make all the difference.

He was at the church standing in line and waiting his turn for the shower. A petite lady named Michelle looked around and picked out our homeless guy (he looked dirtiest?). She approached him and said, "You look like you need a hug." He protested that he had not showered or changed his clothes in three months and that he was really smelly. She grabbed him and hugged him anyway and then said, "Jesus loves you."

At that moment, something clicked for this guy. All his past pain and bad decisions seemed to melt away. That Michelle would accept him in the state he was in was transformative for him. She showed godly generosity. "It just clicked" is the way he describes it. It has kept on clicking to this day. As a result, he eventually became a Christian and is now an ordained minister. All this is because a lady with godlike generosity hugged a stinky, dirty, three-time loser of a drug addict and told him, "Jesus loves you."[2]

So, Jesus taught generous forgiveness; we should catch the spirit of such living for ourselves. It is very interesting—to return to the story of Comrade Duch—that in Cambodia, which is mostly Buddhist, a mass murderer like him would expect to take a thousand reincarnations to get rid of such bad karma. He would have to suffer over and over to pay for such evil. But in Christ, the suffering has already been done; the evil has already been paid for. What would be a thousand terrible reincarnations in Buddhism is a moment of genuine repentance in Christ. Now that's generous forgiveness!

One of my favorite novels of all time is *Les Misérables*. The main character, Jean Valjean, is interesting enough, but the police detective, Javert, is a real study. He hounds Jean Valjean throughout his life, unrelenting in his determination to catch him and return him to prison—for the crime of stealing a loaf of bread! But, finally, Javert must admit that Jean Valjean is a good man. He does not deserve to go to prison. Yet Javert is not a forgiving person. He cannot just let him go. So, he commits suicide by jumping into a river and drowning himself. Now that's a guy who really carries a grudge! He would rather kill himself than forgive. Don't be that way. If God has forgiven, who are we to refuse?

Generous forgiveness: truly a divine character trait. God's grace and compassion are unfair but amazing when we receive them.

DISCUSSION QUESTIONS

1. Why do you think some Christians find it difficult to accept that sinners like serial murderers can be forgiven?

2. How does our understanding (or misunderstanding) of God's forgiveness affect the way we relate to God?

3. What should be the church's teaching on the interaction between God's grace and the expectation of a transformed life? Can we be too casual about grace and ignore the need to press on toward spiritual growth?

4. Does it ever make you angry to think that extremely sinful and criminal persons repent at the last minute?

GOING DEEPER

There is an interesting story in the rabbinic literature that is similar to this parable, but the point is strikingly different:

> It is like a king who hired many laborers. But one was outstanding in his work. What did the king do? He took him away and walked around with him. When it was evening, the laborers came to receive their pay, and he gave him, with them, the full amount of his wage. Then the laborers protested and said, "We have worked the whole day, and this man has worked only two hours." Then the king said, "This man has done more in two hours than you have done in the whole day." (j. Berakot 2.7)[3]

As one New Testament scholar[4] noted—in comparing this rabbinic story with Jesus's parable—in the rabbinic story, the laborer received the same pay because he could do more than the others in a shorter period of time. He did the same work (actually more) but in less time. But in Jesus's parable, it is entirely the generosity of the vineyard owner that brought about the same pay for the one-hour workers and the others. The first story teaches that some do more good things with their lives—even though on this earth a short time—than others who live a long life. But Jesus's parable teaches us about God's amazing (and unfair) grace. God is generous with his forgiveness.

Jesus's parables often picture for us the conditions of life in Palestine in his day. There were many landless workers, day laborers, like those in this parable who sought some work each day. Most of them had no skills as such. They simply had their labor. They might pick fruit, like those in this parable, or work in the fields weeding, plowing, and threshing. Sometimes they carried heavy burdens. Obviously, this kind of work was seasonal. Their only income was the daily wage, but if there was no daily wage, either because the work was out of season or because there were so many day laborers looking for work that there was not enough work to go around, then the family was in trouble. And heaven help the family if the husband/father became too sick to work or broke a leg. It was not acceptable for women to "take a job," except as a midwife or a mourner. The family was stuck with the money the father could earn.

The daily wage of one denarius was the average. Some received much less (as low as 1/24 denarius per day) and others more at the peak season (two or three denarii) when fruit had to be picked quickly to avoid spoilage. The day laborers were the lowest-class persons in Palestine in the time of Jesus. They were even poorer and less cared for than the slaves.

These poor laborers were taken advantage of at every opportunity. Landowners would often try to pay them below the rate of one denarius during harvest time. More insidiously, the landowners would often delay paying their daily wage or not pay it at all (see James 5:4). Or, sometimes, a landowner would force a man's children to glean behind him when he harvested, evidently hoping to gain a little more for the same daily wage.[5]

Their life was unbelievably hard. One way for us to tell now how hard their life was is to examine the bones of some of these people. The remains of one man, for example, who died at age twenty-two, showed that he had done hard physical labor with his hands all his life. He had also gone barefooted (on the rocky ground of Palestine!) all his life. He was evidently too poor to afford a pair of sandals. Another man, who had died at age sixty-five, had also done hard labor. He had carried heavy burdens all his life, causing significant structural damage to his skeletal frame, especially to his shoulders and legs.[6] These are the people depicted in Jesus's parable of the unfair God. You can see why the others complained about unfair treatment. They expected to be cheated constantly. But what they could not seem to process was that some "landowners" (God) were amazingly generous. Is it an accident that Jesus selected the poorest of the poor to illustrate God's shocking generosity?

NOTES

[1] See the story in Strobel, *The Case for Grace.*

[2] The story is in Strobel, *The Case for Grace.*

[3] Quoted in Fiensy, *Message and Ministry of Jesus.*

[4] A. M. Hunter, *Interpreting the Parables* (Louisville: Westminster John Knox, 1976).

[5] On the day laborer, see Fiensy, *The Social History of Palestine in the Herodian Period.*

[6] See Fiensy, *The Archaeology of Daily Life.*

4

LEAVE SKUNKS ALONE

Matt. 18:23–35

A grizzly bear emerged from the woods, approached some standing garbage cans, tipped them over, and began feeding on the garbage. From the woods, many pairs of small eyes watched enviously, but none of the little animals dared challenge the bear for his food. But suddenly a small, furry creature trotted toward the turned-over garbage cans. The bear watched the small animal approach and allowed it to feed alongside himself. It was a skunk. Now the bear could have seriously injured or even killed the skunk with one mighty blow of its paw or crushed its tiny head with its powerful jaws. But would it have been worth it? The bear knew, either by instinct or experience, that it would suffer a nauseating smell on its fur for weeks if it did that. It just wouldn't be worth it. So, the bear tolerated the skunk but allowed no other animal to feed from his trash cans.[1]

There are many two-legged skunks out there. When they harm you or slander you, you can try to get revenge. But is it really worth it? Won't you wind up paying more for your revenge than they will in terms of your character and peace of mind? Some of the best advice I have ever read goes like this: If bad people hurt you, stay away from them, but don't try to get even. You will only hurt yourself.[2]

Jesus's parable is about skunks. They will hurt your career, your family, your reputation, maybe even your health. But will you make it your life's obsession from now on to hurt back? What sort of life is that?

The parable arises in the course of Jesus's teaching about forgiveness. I picture Peter listening to one of Jesus's many teachings on forgiveness (for example, Mark 11:25; Matt. 6:12, 14–15), scratching his head, and then asking the question: "Lord, how many times do I have to forgive skunks? Seven times?"

Certainly, forgiving hurtful people seven times seems like a lot of grace. So, we might say that Peter has been more than generous. But Jesus's answer is a stunner: "No, not seven times but seventy-seven times."[3] In other words, keep forgiving, because that's what the people of God do. Jesus wants his disciples to be known for their forgiveness.

The exchange between Peter and Jesus leads to Jesus's parable of the unforgiving servant. The story begins about a servant who had swiped his credit card so much—so to speak—that he had amassed a debt of ten thousand talents. A talent is a weight of money. One talent equaled around six thousand silver denarii.[4] So, ten thousand talents amounted to sixty million denarii, an enormous sum. The entire annual income of King Herod the Great was one thousand talents. This sum was ten times that! I calculate the buying power of this sum as four billion US dollars today.

The indebted servant is brought before the master and obviously cannot pay the debt. The master orders that he, his wife, and his children be sold into slavery and that every other item (house, land, movable property) be sold to help defray the debt. At this, the man begs for patience. He promises to pay off the loan, given enough time. But now a shocking thing happens. Surprisingly, the master forgives the debt. He simply cancels it. He does not say, "Well, I can give you more time to pay it off." He does not demand a big favor someday in return for canceling the debt. He merely cancels the debt. Amazing grace!

Here is that Greek word (verse 27) we introduced in Chapter One: *splagchnizomai,* "showing compassion." The servant asked for patience; the estate owner instead gave him compassion. The servant asked for some tolerance, and he said he would eventually—not realistically—pay off the debt. The owner just decided to forget the whole thing out of an overwhelming sense of compassion.

Of course, in the parable, the master—the creditor—represents God, the debtor represents all of us, and debt is our sin. This amazing grace is explained in more theological language by Paul in Romans:

- "We are justified free of charge by his grace through the redemption that came by Jesus Christ" (Rom. 3:24).
- "Since we have been justified by his blood, how much more shall we be saved from God's wrath?" (Rom. 5:9).

The point of the parable is that God has forgiven us our sins, as the old hymn says:

Sing it o'er and o'er again
Christ receiveth sinful men.
Make the message clear and plain
Christ receiveth sinful men.[5]

So far, so good. But then in an amazing act of ingratitude and selfishness, the debtor goes out and finds his own debtor. This ungrateful debtor reminds me of a time when we sought to expand our staff at a church. We interviewed a man who had some weaknesses and liabilities. Many didn't want to hire him. We did not agree with everything he was maintaining, and his attitude needed some work. Nonetheless, I argued that if we shepherded him and mentored him, he could add to our ministry. So, we hired him. We told him that we did not agree with everything he was peddling, but we wanted to give him a chance. But then in an irritating act of ingratitude and arrogance, when we interviewed for the next position, this first guy was very judgmental and stubborn. He told the second guy, who was a great candidate, that he would oppose him and do everything he could to prevent his being hired. I couldn't believe it! We had extended grace to the first guy to give him a chance. But he had zero grace for anybody else. How do you explain that kind of attitude?

So, our first debtor has a debtor of his own. Some guy owes him one hundred denarii. Remember, the first debtor owed ten thousand talents (sixty million denarii = four billion dollars). This guy owes him one hundred denarii, which, as I calculate in contemporary American buying power, is roughly seven thousand dollars. Now, seven thousand dollars is not a trivial debt. If someone owed me that, I would need it back eventually. This amount is not nothing, and that means that when people hurt us, God does not consider the hurt insignificant or trivial. It is important to us. But the point is that seven thousand dollars and four billion dollars are hardly comparable.

If you live very long, someone will hurt you. It is only a matter of time. To make matters worse, sometimes the hurter will be one of your family members. At other times, it may be someone in the church. It may be your closest friend. People you least expect to hurt you may hurt you. It seems to make the pain more intense when that happens. But Jesus's parable is about letting go of the anger and hatred which we naturally feel at those times. Long-term resentment harms us physically, emotionally, and especially spiritually. God is the God of forgiveness. Forgiveness is at the heart of the Christian faith. We are called to be forgivers. That calling is the most difficult one.

Just ask Everett Worthington. He is not only a psychologist but a sufferer. After his mother was murdered, he entered a painful period in which he struggled with anger for the murderer. Finally, he and his two siblings decided they had to forgive. He has since spent years studying the health effects of retaining anger as opposed to forgiving. Anger has a pronounced negative effect on our health. It increases stress and spikes our chances of heart trouble. Even among those in very high-stress jobs, if they are forgiving persons, the stress does not seem to hurt them. Forgiveness is not only a beautiful thing spiritually but adds years to your life.[6]

Okay, but how do we do that? Let me suggest four steps toward forgiveness.[7]

First, decide that you *want* to forgive. Now I am not suggesting that you can forgive instantly by deciding this. Forgiveness takes time; it is a process, sometimes a long process. But you can decide that you want to begin the process. If the process takes you months or even years, don't feel bad about yourself. A really severe hurt will take time.

I read a newspaper story about a man injured in a convenience store robbery several years ago. The robber had shot the cashier and left him paralyzed from the waist down. The journalist doing the story asked the former cashier, now in a wheelchair, if he had forgiven the assailant. "I wake up every morning," the cashier replied, "and have to forgive him all over again." Yes, that's how forgiveness goes. But one day, the cashier will not have to go through this painful process anymore. His forgiveness will be completed. First, decide that you want to forgive.

Second, pray earnestly for the ability to forgive. I really wonder if forgiving a terrible wrong is a human possibility. We humans naturally want revenge. We naturally turn to hatred when wronged egregiously. I was amazed in 2015 when Dylann Roof was being arraigned in court after his murder of nine Christians at a Wednesday night prayer service at the Emanuel African Methodist Episcopal Church in South Carolina. At the arraignment, relatives of the nine slain persons were allowed to address the perpetrator. One after the other said something like the following: "You hurt me terribly when you killed my mother (or brother, or husband, or wife), but Christ commands me to forgive you, and so I do."[8] Wow! How does anyone do that? I just don't think that kind of forgiveness is a human possibility. Pray for the ability to forgive.

Third, find some way to verbalize your forgiveness. It may be that you tell the offender that you forgive. But be careful here. Skunks don't want your forgiveness and certainly don't want you to tell them you have forgiven them. That implies that you think they have done something wrong (and of course, they have). So, you probably need to verbalize the forgiveness to someone else, maybe a spouse, a friend, or a pastor.

An American couple on vacation in Italy in the summer of 2018 found a unique way to verbalize their forgiveness. The husband was suffering from terminal cancer. This was to be their last vacation together, their beautiful memory in the final months of the husband's life. But when they arrived in Venice, someone picked the man's pocket and stole his cash, credit card, and debit card. At first, they were incensed that someone would ruin their time together. But eventually they calmed down and decided to forgive. To express this, they penned an open letter and gave it to the local newspaper. Soon the open letter was printed all over Italy. It read as follows:

> To the person who stole my wallet. I know you probably won't read this and I know you may not care. We arrived in your beautiful city on 14 July (2018). I became your next victim. This is my last trip with my wife. I'm dying from cancer. You left me with no money and no credit cards. Imagine for only a moment what this does to your victim. I have been praying for forgiveness. I also pray for you. Turn away from your sin which hurts innocent people. I forgive you. Michael Veley, U.S.A.[9]

Fourth, think often of God's forgiveness for you. It helps. We all have feet of clay. We all have sinned. We all have hurt someone, either unintentionally or—even at times—intentionally. But God in his infinite grace forgives us. It helps to think about that grace. The first debtor in the parable did not think about what the master had forgiven him; he only thought about what the second debtor owed.

So, this is my strategy for forgiveness. But what is forgiveness? First, let me state what I think forgiveness is *not*. Forgiveness is not forgetting all about it. When someone hurts you deeply, you can't just forget about it. "I lost my arm somehow ten years ago but now can't remember how it happened." That just makes no sense. You will never forget that Billy X attacked you with a meat cleaver and cut your arm off. It's just unrealistic to expect people to forget all about their deep hurts. But you can stop replaying the event in your mind all the time. Refuse to crank up the video player day after day to relive the terrible moment. Refuse to allow this event to define you and haunt your every waking moment. There will be times, of course, when the video just comes on by itself. Something in your current experience will trigger it. You can't help that. But try not to intentionally replay the scene over and over. You can't really forget the event, but you can refuse to let it into your thoughts all the time.

Forgiveness is also not letting criminals go. Even though the relatives of the tragic victims forgave Dylann Roof, he is not free to leave prison. Criminals might commit the crime again. It would be irresponsible, if not criminal itself, to release a criminal just because the victim had found the moral courage to forgive. Forgive the criminal personally but hold him or her responsible for the crime.

Finally, forgiveness is not necessarily trusting that person again. It might mean that, but it also might not. Let's say someone harms your child in any way. You might, after much prayer, find a way to offer forgiveness, but please don't ever let that person be alone with your child again. Being forgiven doesn't necessarily earn the right to be trusted. We must always use good sense.

Okay, those three things define what forgiving is not. So, what is it? First of all, I believe forgiving is letting go of hatred and the desire for revenge. In one of my favorite speeches, Martin Luther King Jr. said, "I don't hate anybody. I've seen what hatred can do to a person. Hate is too great a burden to bear." And so it is. Carrying around a load of hatred all your life will weigh you down. You need to let it go.

Second, forgiving is celebrating the future and not being enslaved to the past. When we hate our enemies, we give them power over us; over our sleep, our appetite, blood pressure, health, and happiness. Our hatred does not hurt them; it hurts us. Don't let a past injury ruin the rest of your life. Don't let the injury decide how you will live from now on. Live for the future.

Third, forgiveness is not something you do once or twice in your lifetime; it is a new spiritual openness. Again, Martin Luther King Jr. said: "Forgiveness is not an occasional act. It is a constant attitude." It is not just something we push through after the one or two great hurts of our lifetime; it is learning a great truth about God and about our calling as Christians: forgiveness is the heart and soul of Jesus's ethic and our most difficult calling in life.

Finally, forgiving means finding the amazing power of love. I'm convinced you can't understand the power of love until you learn to love someone who is truly unlovable. Most striking was the statement of forgiveness made by Brandt Jean on October 3, 2019. Brandt's brother had been killed by an off-duty policewoman who thought he was in her apartment (it turned out, she was actually in *his* apartment). She was sentenced to ten years in prison. After the sentencing, Brandt asked the judge if he could give the defendant a hug. Then he said the remarkable words: He didn't want her to go to prison, and he forgave her.[10] How on earth does someone do that? Not by his or her will alone. The kind of person who can do that is someone who has learned about love and grace.

Jesus wants his disciples to be forgiveness warriors. That kind of life is not easy. The Christian life is not for wimps. To forgive a deep hurt is the most difficult thing you will ever do. But in doing that, you truly find the heart of God. This is the essence of what the Christian faith is all about.

Christian forgiveness today is wonderfully modeled around the world. In the summer of 2018, pastor Andrew Brunson, for twenty-five years the minister of the Izmir Resurrection Church in Turkey, endured his third trial for terrorism. He had been accused two years earlier of plotting with terrorists and of participating in an attempted coup in Turkey. Even though there was no evidence against him, his trials had been continued. At his third trial, he was given the opportunity to speak. He said, "My faith teaches me to forgive, so I forgive those who testified against me." With this statement, Pastor Brunson modeled for us what it means to be a disciple of Jesus, and he followed in Jesus's own footsteps when he prayed from the cross, “Father forgive them, for they do not know what they are doing” (Luke 23:34).

So, if you have a burden of anger you are carrying, I hope you can find a way to let it go. It really is too much for you to bear for the rest of your life. And I pray, if you are working through forgiving, that my counsel here will be of some help.

DISCUSSION QUESTIONS

1. Do you find it easy to forgive or especially difficult? Why do you think some can forgive more easily than others?

2. When you are hurt or offended, what sort of process do you go through to heal?

3. Are you able to forget the offense as well as forgive it? Do you find it difficult to turn off the video of the hurt?

4. How do you think people like Pastor Brunson find the moral strength to forgive their enemies?

GOING DEEPER

For examples of selling someone and his family into slavery because of debts, see the following: "A woman, the wife of a member of the prophetic guild, pleaded with Elisha. She said, 'Your servant, my husband, has died. You know that your servant reverenced the LORD. But the creditor came and took two of my sons for slaves'" (2 Kings 4:1). "There was a loud complaint of the people and their wives to their kinfolk in Judah. Some said, 'We've had to give our fields and vineyards—even our daughters!—as a pledge so we could get grain in the famine . . . and now we are forcing our sons and daughters into slavery'" (Neh. 5:1, 3, 5b).

The rabbinic sources also knew of selling family members to cover a debt. There is a parable in which a man owed a large wheat debt to a king. The king seized all the children of the house and sold them off as repayment on the loan (*Sifre* Deuteronomy 26). The Mishnah ruled that a man and all his children could be sold for a debt, but not a woman (m. Sotah 3:8; m. Gittin 4:9), evidently to prohibit prostitution. What Jesus is describing in his parable happened every day in his time. Imagine the horrors for the children.

In the Old Testament period, both pre-exilic and post-exilic, and in the time of Jesus, selling one's children into slavery or having them confiscated to cover a debt was common. It was also common throughout the Middle East and Greco-Roman world. Tragically—and horrifyingly—in times of danger the poorest families had only one resource: the children. A cruel creditor would take those "resources" in a heartbeat. But our first creditor in the parable, unlike the king in the rabbinic parable, was moved by compassion.

The average day laborer could earn around one denarius per day (see Chapter Three). So, the second debtor owed the equivalent of one hundred days' work. That is not a trivial sum. Historians have calculated that the average day laborer could work around 200 days per year (because of Sabbaths, bad weather, and seasonal unavailability). Thus, the worker (second debtor) owed a half year's wages. When we see it that way, we realize it is a serious sum, but pales in comparison. The first debtor owed sixty million days' work, an astronomical sum.[11]

The reference to seven in verse 21 ("forgive seven times") is a mirror image (opposite) of the warning against harming Cain ("The LORD said to him, 'Therefore, anyone killing Cain will be avenged seven times'"; Gen. 4:15) and Lamech's boast ("If Cain will be avenged seven times, Lamech will be avenged seventy-seven times"; Gen. 4:24). The Genesis texts warn of a vengeance of seven times and seventy-seven times; the parable speaks of seven times (and then some) of forgiving.

NOTES

[1] This illustration is taken from Dale Carnegie, *How to Stop Worrying and Start Living* (New York: Simon and Schuster, 1950).

[2] Carnegie, *How to Stop Worrying.*

[3] One ancient manuscript reads "seventy times seven." But we get the picture either way. Keep on forgiving.

[4] Danker, *Greek-English Lexicon.*

[5] Hymn by Erdmann Neumeister (1718); Translator: Frances Bevan (1899).

[6] Jacqueline Howard, "Forgiveness and Your Health: What Science Says about the Benefits," *CNN*, June 5, 2019, www.cnn.com/2019/06/05/health/forgiveness-health-explainer/index.html.

[7] Compare my steps with the four steps in a 2019 article in the *New York Times*: (1) Forgiveness is for you, not the offender. (2) Do it now. (3) It's about freeing yourself. (4) Begin with calming yourself down from the anger. See Tim Herrera, "Let Go of Your Grudges. They're Doing You No Good," *New York Times*, May 19, 2019, www.nytimes.com/2019/05/19/smarter-living/let-go-of-your-grudges-theyre-doing-you-no-good.html.

[8] Mark Berman, "'I Forgive You.' Relatives of Charleston Church Shooting Victims Address Dylann Roof," *Washington Post*, June 19, 2015, www.washingtonpost.com/news/post-nation/wp/2015/06/19/i-forgive-you-relatives-of-charleston-church-victims-address-dylann-roof/.

[9] Farnoush Amiri, "Terminally Ill American Robbed on Italian Vacation, Pens 'Open Letter' Forgiving Thief," NBC News, July 19, 2018, www.nbcnews.com/news/world/terminally-ill-american-robbed-italian-vacation-pens-open-letter-forgiving-n892816.

[10] Darran Simon, "Botham Jean's Brother Hugs the Former Police Officer Who Killed Him," *CNN*, October 3, 2019, www.cnn.com/2019/10/02/us/botham-jean-brother-amber-guyger-hug/index.html.

[11] See Fiensy, *Social History of Palestine in the Herodian Period.*

5

TIME FOR A SOIL TEST

Mark 4:1–9 and 13–20

When you live in Eastern Kentucky, you have to make certain adjustments to enter into gardening. Well, I'm not much of a gardener myself. But when we bought our first house with a spacious backyard, my wife wanted a garden. So, I tried to accommodate her. To me, doing gardening involves hiring some guy with a tractor to come and plow up an area we have marked off. Then he comes back in a week and pulls a disc over it. Finally, I make a few rows with a hoe and my wife plants the seed. After that, I wait for it to happen.

The first year, the garden did extremely well. We had zucchini the size of watermelons. The next year, it was not so spectacular. The third year, it looked like a Middle Eastern desert. Each year, we used the same quality of seed. The difference was the soil. I took a soil sample to the local agricultural adviser, and he told me that our soil, typical for Eastern Kentucky, was unusually acidic. We needed a lot of fertilizer and lime. That's the lesson from gardening in this part of the country. You need a soil test.

Christians also need a soil test from time to time. Commentators commonly call this parable the Parable of the Sower. But it really is the Parable of the Four Soils.[1] The soils are the point. The "soil" refers to our attitudes, our first loves (God or something else?), and our behavior. All of us represent some kind of "soil." In this parable, Jesus talks about four kinds of soil. These are the four main types of people that hear the gospel and respond to it based on their priorities (loves) and principles. Which type of soil are you?

Three Christian ladies died and stood before St. Peter to await entry into heaven. Peter tells them he has some important business to do and asks them to wait in line. Finally, he calls the first lady into his office. He apologizes for the wait. "Oh, I don't mind," answers the first lady. "I'm just thrilled to be in heaven. I'll wait as long as you want me to." Peter is pleased to hear this response. He says, "Great. Just answer one question and then we can process your entry into the pearly gates. Spell *God*." The lady spells *God* and is immediately ushered into heaven. Peter goes outside and invites the second lady into his office. He apologizes for the wait. The lady answers, "I don't mind. The thrill of seeing God face to face makes it worth it all. I'll wait a thousand years if I have to." Peter is very pleased to hear this and again asks her to spell the word *God*. She spells it and enters heaven. He then goes to the third lady. He invites her into his office and apologizes for the wait. But this lady complains: "It was really rude. I've had to wait in lines all my life on earth. And then, I get to heaven and what do I find? More lines! You expect me to wait in line for heaven? I won't stand for it!" Peter apologizes once again and says, "Sorry. If you can just spell one word, we'll get you processed and immediately into heaven. Spell the word *Czechoslovakia*."[2]

Notice in the joke, the reward is the same (heaven), the reception by Peter is the same, and the wait is the same. But one lady is impatient and feeling entitled. The others are humble and grateful. In the parable, the four soils represent four personality types. The seed is the Word of God. Notice that the seed is the same in each case. It is the soil that changes. The Word of God is the same for each of us, but we receive it and process it differently depending on our prejudices, priorities, and life habits. You see, people experience things differently, though the experience may be the same. An old saying is "the same sun that melts the wax hardens the clay." Or again, life can be a grindstone: it grinds down some people but polishes others. The sun is the same and the grindstone is the same, but those who receive them are different. Let's look at each type of personality or character.

The first soil (character type) represents those persons with a **Hard Heart**. Jesus says the seed falls on the path (hardened by many footsteps), and the birds (Satan) come and eat it almost immediately. These are people who hear the word but do not ever believe. Their hearts never know repentance, sorrow for sin, or conversion. They are hard.

What makes people this hard? Some are proud. They think religion is for children and adults who are still children in their minds. They are grown up and have no time or inclination for "fairy tales."

Others have hard hearts because they simply love their lifestyle too much. They are immersed in themselves and their "fun" and think faith in God might put a damper on it. They want to live for their pleasures: sex, gambling, drink, drugs, music, etc. Life for them is one string of pleasures after another. It holds no mystery, no sense of awe, no fear of God, just pleasure. Life is a game, a joke, a party. They cannot be serious about it. Oh, maybe someday they will take a serious look at it, but not now. Now is for playing. So, when rather stern-looking people ask them about their eternal destiny, they freak out and say to themselves, "This guy or woman is creepy. What do I care about this?"

Still others' hearts become hard and they do not accept the Word because of their upbringing. They have been raised in a totally secular family and have never been taught to think about spiritual issues. They might have some questions in the back of their minds about things, but their university professors maintained (at least they said it in class) that these things do not matter, that spiritual entities and issues do not exist anyway, and that to dwell on them is childish and naïve. These are secular people. And so, when the Word is taught, they are like pavement trying to grow seed. It simply can't be done—unless God intervenes (which he often does).

Finally, others have developed hard hearts because they have had bad experiences. They grew up in an abusive family or in an abusive church. There is such a thing as spiritual abuse, such as when persons in authority positions (pastors, teachers, and parents) exploit and manipulate children and adults with ecclesiastical clout. They threaten them with hell if they disagree with them; they denounce their behavior loudly from the pulpit; they skin them alive in sermons and Sunday school lessons. These persons were beaten up in their childhood and continue feeling that way into adulthood. To them, belief in Christ involves being hammered on each Sunday. The Christian faith is not a celebration of God's goodness but a burden to be borne, to be endured. No wonder their hearts become hardened. The first soil is the path, and that represents hard-hearted persons.

The second soil represents persons of **Shallow Heart**. Jesus says that the seed fell on the rocky places. There were rocks there, but very little soil. Oh, sure, the seed germinated and grew up rather quickly, but because there was so little soil, the roots did not grow very deeply in the ground. When the summer sun began to shine every day, the plants withered. There was not enough soil and thus not enough moisture in the soil to sustain the plant.

These persons, says Jesus in his interpretation, are those who hear the gospel and receive it joyfully, but when the going gets tough, they give it up. They endure a hardship of some kind (sickness, loss of a loved one) or are persecuted for their faith. They give it up rather quickly and easily because they have no depth of faith. These persons are enthusiastic but shallow. They are like friends who hang out with you as long as you are a fun person. But when you go through suffering, many of them will withdraw. It is too uncomfortable for them to be around suffering.

We have all known persons who make dramatic conversions only to fall away in a relatively short time. Movie stars often do this. They make the news because of their well-publicized finding religion. Then, a year later, they might be caught in a scandal of some sort. Their behavior did not really change. They felt good for a while; felt euphoric and clean. Let's face it, religious conversion feels good. It is a spiritual and emotional high. But then, they soon returned to their old habits. Living the life does not always feel good. It is often a life of discipline and growth. It's like the difference between the honeymoon and the daily grind in a marriage. A real marriage involves caring for your spouse when she or he is sick; overlooking hurts; engaging in conflict and settling conflict in a loving way; admitting mistakes and apologizing. Real marriage is not a Hallmark movie every day (well, it is sometimes). It is a commitment to the love of your life.

There was a lady in my home church who, each year when we had our fall revival (yes, we had one every fall), would "rededicate" her life. She would weep and lament her past sins and promise reformation. Then, we did not see her again for the rest of the year. As I look back, I wonder if we should have ministered to her more compassionately. She obviously had a behavior pattern that she simply could not overcome. She wanted to but could not. So, each year, the re-conversion was followed by the relapse. She felt better about herself for a while, but not for long. It soon became too difficult to keep up the change and she was back.

The old saying is, "Some people never grow up. They just grow old." Some persons never realize that life is serious. They never grasp that we have eternal decisions to make and stick with. In their lives, there is no deep confrontation with sin and repentance. They just want to feel good.

These people are the shallow soil. They have not grown in Christ. They have remained babies in the Lord, so to speak, and so, when trouble comes—and it will inevitably come—they fall back into their old habits and behaviors. Jesus says literally, "They stumble." In other words, like a toddler learning to walk, who falls frequently because of unsteadiness, they tumble over. It's easy to fall when you never grow. When you remain in the toddler phase, you can fall easily.

How does growth come? It comes by prayer, by serious study of the Word, and by fellowshipping and learning from other people of God. The second soil represents people of shallow heart.

The third soil represents persons of **Worldly Heart**. In this soil, the good seed falls among the thorns. When the grain grows up, the thorns choke it and kill it. The thorns stand for three things Jesus mentions in his interpretation: the worries of this life, the deceit of wealth, and the desires for other things.

The worries of this life can interfere with our spiritual growth (in other words, with the growth of the plant). "How am I going to make the house payment? How can I afford another car since the junk heap I'm driving now is so unreliable? I'm too busy with my job to think about church. Church is the last thing I can give attention to now. Don't bother me with this! I'm just trying to live week by week." The worries of life can really do a job on our receptivity to the Word of God.

So can the deceit of wealth. Other persons want desperately to be wealthy. Some people, especially young people, long to be billionaires. Wealth becomes such an obsession they begin to forget about God. They are deadly earnest about this goal. They will neglect their marriage, their children, and their own health in order to accomplish this goal. Naturally, their spiritual life is soon neglected.

Wealth is such a compelling temptation. We want to live like the rich and famous. We want multiple mansions, yachts, exotic vacations, designer clothes, people fighting to be near us and perhaps interview us. We want to be among the upper 1 percent on the planet. I've known men and women who were consumed by this dream. Sometimes it is not businesspersons but Christian gospel musicians. The number of Christian vocalists and instrumentalists that have gotten caught up in the glitz of fame is staggering. They often commit adultery, get into drugs, and, in general, betray their ministry. Their heads were turned by the deceit of wealth.

It's deceitful because wealth lies to us. It promises what it can never deliver. We come to think, "If only I had a million dollars—or ten million, or a hundred million, or a billion—everything would be super." That is a lie, of course. The most pathetic people are those who have everything to live with but nothing to live for.

And then, there are "the desires for other things." Maybe the problem is not wealth per se but "other things." Maybe a person's problem is success or fame. Maybe this person lives for their career, house, car, hobby, wardrobe, good looks, or prestige. They will take the money that comes with those things, naturally, but the money is not the main thing. They just must be famous or they must climb the corporate ladder. They worship success. But here is the spiritual lesson we all must learn, and it is a difficult one: We must never desire anything more than we desire God. He is our life, our joy, our happiness, our peace, and our purpose for living. The third soil represents persons of worldly heart.

The fourth and final soil represents people with an **Open Heart**. In this case, the seed (the Word) fell on the good soil and it produced plenty. Notice some things about the fourth soil: The soil produced a variety of yields. In addition, the good soil brought forth fruit. Some soil produced thirtyfold, some sixtyfold, and some a hundredfold. Not all good soil yields identical fruit. You don't need to compete with other Christians in the amount of fruit you produce. The idea is just to produce some. God does not judge you on the number of bushels, so to speak.

Regardless of the quantity, the good soil did bring forth a harvest. I want to suggest that this fruit is manifest in the Christian life in two ways. First, it is growth in character (the love, joy, peace, patience, self-control, etc., of Gal. 5:22–23). We advance in our own sanctification, in our own integrity, and in our own spirituality. The Christian life is a journey, a process, and we are engaged in it. We do not reach the end of the journey in this life, but we stay on the road. We keep advancing—or I should say, letting the Holy Spirit lead us forward.

Second, the fruit means, I suggest, actual works of love such as witnessing, helping the poor, comforting the depressed and grieving, serving as a Sunday school teacher or small group leader, and serving as a church officer. The fruit is not only our personal sanctification but also our overt works of love. Bearing fruit means you *do* something.

So the question is: Are you producing fruit? Ultimately only you and God know the answer to this question. Are you growing in your faith? Are you helping others in the name of Christ? As it has been said, ultimately, the true test of a Christian is fruit, not foliage. Foliage can mask what the plant is actually doing. Sometimes it looks like it must be doing great things, but we find little to no fruit on it. Likewise, church busyness can look like we are producing fruit, but it may be only a pretense.

How do we start producing fruit? Want it. Pray for it. Be open to it. The Holy Spirit will take over.

There are four soils—that is, four character types or four conditions of the spiritual heart. Which one are you?

DISCUSSION QUESTIONS

1. As in the case of a later study in this book (Chapter Seven on Matt. 13:24–30, 37–43), Jesus gives not only the parable but his interpretation of the parable. These are the only two parables in the New Testament where the interpretation is also given. Why do you think Jesus gave the interpretation of this parable?

2. How greatly do the worries of life impede your spiritual growth? What can you do about it?

3. We all rejoice in our own and other people's spiritual experiences. How can we help to turn those experiences into real commitment?

4. In what way does the consumer ethic of America and Western Europe interfere with spiritual values and growth?

GOING DEEPER

When they planted a crop in the Middle East in Jesus's day, they scattered the seed everywhere and then came later and plowed it under. The rabbinic literature refers to this process: "the one who sows along the sea, on cliffs, on rocks, or on hard ground . . ."[3] You get the idea that they slung the seed just about anywhere. Of course, they were a little more careful than that, but some seed would necessarily fall in those other places.

Often the birds would be watching as the farmer was scattering seed, only to swoop down and consume it, especially those seeds that stood out on a hard-packed pathway. There is a famous story—certainly apocryphal but illustrating the technology of the time—about Abraham distinguishing himself as a farmer. In the story, Abraham is fourteen years old and figures out something: you have to protect your crop from the birds. His family has planted a crop, and suddenly a cloud of crows descended on the field (probably a usual event). But Abraham ran out onto the field and scattered the crows. All day, every day he did this (the story says he had to do it seventy times a day) in order to allow the seeds to germinate. This action was evidently a new idea to the local residents of Mesopotamia where Abraham grew up. They began to hire him to help them keep away the birds from their planted fields.[4] It is kind of a funny story to us. But it does illustrate the dire threat to livelihood and subsistence that birds could be.

Throughout the summer—from April to October—it seldom rains a drop. Thus, whatever moisture the plants can get must already be in the soil. It stands to reason that deep soil will hold more moisture than shallow soil.

Huge thorn bushes are ubiquitous in Israel. They seem to grow easily in that soil and remain healthy through the dry summer months.

A harvest of thirty times your seed would be astounding in the ancient world (not to mention sixty or one hundred times). Generally, they received five times the crop from the planted seed. One rabbinic text reads: "A (bushel of grain sowed) in a field in Judea yielded five bushels."[5] Yields of thirty, sixty, and one hundred times the seed planted would have been unthinkable. Why do you think Jesus gave such exaggerated yields in the parable?

Finally, one commentator—who grew up in Palestine in the early twentieth century—observed that Jesus did not say anything about other common threats to the crop; namely, the hot east winds (called the *sirocco* or *ḥamsin*) and locusts.[6] Why leave these out? He had what he needed to make his theological and ethical lesson.

NOTES

[1] See R. C. Foster, *Studies in the Life of Christ* (Joplin, MO: College Press, 1995): "It might have been called 'The Parable of the Soils.'" See also Capon, *Kingdom, Grace, Judgment*.

[2] King Duncan and Angela Akers, *Amusing Grace* (Knoxville, TN: Seven Worlds Corporation, 1993).

[3] j. Kilaim 1, 27b. Translation in Hermann Strack and Paul Billerbeck, *Kommentar zum Neuen Testament aus Talmud und Midrasch* (Munich: Beck, 1922), vol. 1.

[4] The story is in the apocryphal Book of Jubilees.

[5] See Fiensy, *The Social History of Palestine in the Herodian Period.*

[6] Jeremias, *Parables.*

6

"TWO WENT UP TO PRAY" —WELL, ACTUALLY, ONLY ONE PRAYED

Luke 18:9–14

Once the royal lion decided to go around the jungle and strut his power. He grabbed the tiger and demanded, "Who is the king of the jungle?" The tiger responded, "You are, of course." Then he grabbed a bear by the throat and asked, "Who is the king of the jungle?" The bear answered likewise, "You are, O mighty lion." Finally, he came to an elephant. He grabbed the elephant by the trunk and growled, "Who is the king of the jungle?" The elephant picked the lion up with his trunk, swung him around a few times, and threw him against a tree trunk. The lion fell to the ground bruised, broken, and bleeding. The lion moaned, "Just because he didn't know the answer, he didn't have to beat me up."

Pride will get you into trouble. You will fall someday. It will lead to your destruction.

At the end of the school year, a fourth-grade teacher decided to give awards not only for the best math student and the best speller but also for the humblest student in the class. There was no doubt who that was: little Billy. So, she called Billy to the front of the class and pronounced him the humblest pupil in the fourth grade. She pinned a gold medal on his shirt that said, "Humblest pupil." But the next day, she took it away from him—because he wore it.

Pride and humility are tricky things. You may think you are not proud, others may think you are not proud, but that does not prove it. Billy was proud after all.

Jesus told this parable to persons who thought they were special to God. They thought they were God's superstars. "Surely, God looks at us every day and smiles," they must have thought to themselves. "We are so much better, so much more moral, so much more spiritual than other people."

So, Jesus told a parable about two who prayed. Two men went up to the temple to pray. But how did they go up to pray? Did they go up in a state of repentance? Were they in awe of the great God? That's the point. One of them did; the other did not.

The first one to pray was a Pharisee. I know what you are thinking: "Well, they were all hypocrites anyway." No, they were not. Jesus denounced some of them for hypocrisy but, surely, we should not think they were all hypocrites. The ancient sources tell us there were six thousand Pharisees in the first century. We can't expect that all of them—or even most of them—were hypocrites. Certainly, some of them were. There are hypocrites in every religion, even in Christianity, even in your own church—perhaps you are one yourself. Oops! Too personal.

No, this guy was probably a paragon of morality and piety. I believe that he spoke the truth in his prayer. He lived a very good life: he did not steal, was not a criminal, and did not commit adultery. He was also very pious (performed religious acts): he fasted twice a week and he tithed his income. This man would be a great church member if he were here today. Every Christian pastor would want him in their congregation. We would all say, "If only I had a church full of people like that Pharisee!" No, Jesus uses him in the parable not because he is a bad guy but because he is an ethical model. To all observing eyes, the guy is perfect.

But in spite of all these moral and pious virtues, the man was rotten inwardly. He was full of himself. He did not really pray to God, did not praise God, did not confess to God his reliance on him, did not acknowledge that all he had and was came from God. Instead, he bragged on himself to God. "He congratulated God in having such a wonderful worshiper as himself."[1] Jesus says that he prayed toward himself. That is, the prayer was not really to God but was to himself.

The tax collector, on the other hand, was no moral superman. He was a rogue, a swindler, a heartless extortionist. Most tax collectors became enormously wealthy by overcharging the poor farmers and day laborers. They put a burden of taxation on the population to enrich themselves. It is no wonder that the ordinary rural folk hated them. Tax collectors were dishonest and greedy. This guy was not a good man.

Yet when he prays, he does not even look up toward God. He is evidently too ashamed. He beats his chest in a sign of mourning. And he only asks God to be merciful to him because he is a sinner. This guy was truly repentant. He prayed to God and acknowledged that he needed grace. Jesus concludes that the second one went to his house "justified" or right with God, not the first one, not the Pharisee.

The sin of pride is called the "Great Sin" by C. S. Lewis. He wrote:

> According to Christian teachers, the essential vice,
> the utmost evil, is Pride. Unchastity, anger, greed,

> drunkenness, and all that, are mere fleabites in comparison: it was through Pride that the devil became the devil. Pride leads to every other vice: it is the complete anti-God state of mind.[2]

Pride is tricky business. Even good, moral people can be susceptible. It can infect your soul and eat away at your devotion to God like a disease. The tricky part is that the more righteous you become, the more tempting pride is for you, just like the Pharisee in the parable. What is pride? Let's define it more carefully.

Pride is, first of all, the sin of competition. As C. S. Lewis writes, a greedy person wants a lot of money (wants it all, really; see Chapter Nine), but a proud person wants *more* money than anybody else. It is not the money itself that the proud person wants; it is the thought of being more powerful or richer than others. A well-known pop singer was being interviewed recently, and the interviewer asked him why he kept up the torrid pace of concerts at his age. The interviewer pointed out that this entertainer already had more money than he could ever spend. The singer replied, "Whoever dies with the most toys wins." In other words, he did not sing for the money; he sang to earn *more* money than others. My question to myself, when I heard his answer, was, "Wins what? What will you win? No one will give you a prize. You will have done all this for nothing. And two years after you die, no one will think of you." That's not winning, folks.

So, pride is essentially competitive. Note how the Pharisee compared himself with the tax collector. "I thank you that I am not like him." He felt superior because he was morally better. Here is the bald truth: whenever you are arrogant about anything—your looks, your wealth, your education, even your morality—you are guilty of the sin of pride. You have no right to be conceited about any of these things. Your looks are an accident of DNA;

your wealth you probably inherited or earned because the right opportunity came along; your education you worked for, but think of how many people on this planet will never have the chance you had to obtain one; and your morality—though commendable—also is not entirely your own doing. If you had been raised in a home where the parents did drugs, engaged in free sex, and committed crimes, do you think your morality would be so easy? Thank God for anything you think makes you "superior."

Second, pride is self-worship. The reason it is so difficult for an arrogant person to be truly dedicated to God—in spite of appearances and in spite of his or her claim—is that the conceited person focuses on self. The godly person focuses on God. You cannot know God as long as you are always worried about your image, your rights, your praise, or your pleasures. This is the reason pride is the ultimate sin, the great sin. We replace God with ourselves; it is the ultimate idolatry. Notice in the parable the Pharisee prayed "toward himself." He does not really pray to the Almighty God.

Third, pride is the primeval sin; it was the sin of the devil: "(A bishop) should not be a new Christian; otherwise, he may get the bighead and make the same mistake as the devil" (1 Tim. 3:6).[3] It is also the archetypical sin among humanity. This was the driving force behind Adam and Eve's sin. They saw that the forbidden fruit not only might be tasty, not only was beautiful, but most importantly, would make them wise like God (Gen. 3:6). The sin appealed to their ego. "Wow! I want to be wise like God!" Pride is the archetypical sin.

Okay, that's what pride is. What does it do? First, it ignores grace. We are all sinners saved by the blood of Jesus Christ. No one should think he or she is God's man or woman and not in need of grace. Arrogant people do not make enough place for the grace they have received in order to be where they are today. These persons think they are special to God. They *are* special to

God, of course, but not more special than anybody else. We are all special to him, just as all of your children and grandchildren are special to you. But the conceited person thinks God favors him or her (or in a twist on this, that God favors their nation) more than others. Here's a news flash: you are not more admired by God or loved by God than any other human being on this planet. We are all special to God. And even more important: Jesus died for us all—you too, dear reader.

Second, arrogance hurts others. A joke I read recently went like this: "I'm not really arrogant; I just don't want to talk to you idiots." It was meant to be a joke, but it speaks a lot of truth. This is probably the way many arrogant people think. Their opinion of themselves and lack of respect for others devalues other people. They see others as unworthy of their attention, their time, their talents. This is the way the Pharisee regarded the tax collector. He thanks God that he is not like "other people," especially the tax collector. But, as I wrote just above: You did not create yourself; you did not redeem yourself. All of us need God. Do not devalue other human beings who were, just like you, created in God's image and who were, just like you, redeemed by the blood of Christ. The Pharisee actually *was* like other people.

Third, pride or conceit makes us unable to say, "I'm sorry." Proud people struggle to ever apologize. To them, apologizing is a sign of weakness.[4] But not only is that attitude offensive to others; it can wreck your career, your marriage, and your spiritual relationship with God. It was said that President Richard Nixon could never admit that he was wrong about anything. Trying to make it through life that way is an impossible task. We all make mistakes; we all are wrong about something once in a while; we all sin. Proud people don't fool anybody. We all know that they are lying to themselves as well as to us. The Pharisee who bragged about himself to God in the parable was not really a perfect person.

It is not right when people are proud of their looks, wealth, social status, education—or even their righteousness. We are all sinners saved by grace; we are all persons of great weaknesses (in addition to our unique talents); we are all created and redeemed by God. We could not do these things for ourselves.

Okay, so what is the antidote to pride? Let me suggest two actions: First admit that we all have it. Again, to quote C. S. Lewis, "The more pride one (has), the more one (dislikes) pride in others."[5] So, if you find arrogance and conceit especially unattractive and irritating when you see it in someone else, it only means that you also are eaten up with it. Only your pride keeps you from admitting it. But to have a relationship with God, we must repent of pride. The old preacher adage is true: "God sends none away empty but those who are full of themselves." The epistle of James admonishes us to humble ourselves before the Lord, and he will lift us up (James 4:10).

So, first of all, admit that you are proud. Second, turn this over to God. Ask God to help you with your problem. Again, C. S. Lewis: "God is not out to hurt our pride; he is out to destroy it."

Decades ago, the *Times* of London ran a series of articles and letters to the editor answering the question: "What's wrong with the world?" G. K. Chesterton, a Christian author, responded: "Dear Sir, I am. Sincerely, G. K. Chesterton."

Billy Graham wrote in his book *World Aflame*[6] about a wealthy, aristocratic man who lived in England in the late Middle Ages. The rich man, as he lay dying, decided that he needed to become a Christian to secure his place in heaven. He called to his servant, whom he knew to be a Christian, and asked what he needed to do to be saved.

The servant responded, "Sir, if you want to be saved, you will have to go to the pigpen, get on your knees in the mud, and say, 'God be merciful to me a sinner.'"

The wealthy man was stunned by such a demand. "I can't do that," he said. "What would the neighbors and servants think of me?" He was evidently too proud to take such a drastic step.

One week passed, and the man's condition worsened. He decided that proud or not, he must go ahead and do what the servant told him to do. Finally, defeated and desperate, he called the servant. He declared that he was ready to go to the pigpen, get on his knees in the stinky mud, and beg God for mercy.

But the servant responded, "Master, you don't really have to go to the pigpen. You just have to be willing."

And so do we. If the pigpen seems too embarrassing and too demeaning—a bridge too far—then we perhaps need to rethink repentance and its opposite, pride, as we stand before God.

DISCUSSION QUESTIONS

1. Do you agree with C. S. Lewis that pride is the "great sin"?

2. Why does pride tempt devoutly religious persons?

3. Is it possible to be arrogant and conceited and not know it?

4. Why do proud people find it so difficult to apologize?

GOING DEEPER

The two evidently went up to pray at the daily offering, which was given at sunrise and in the middle of the afternoon. It was called simply "The Daily (Offering)." In the twice-daily offering, one priest would offer a lamb or calf and another priest would enter the Sanctuary and offer incense (as John the Baptist's father did in Luke 1:8–9). Kenneth Bailey surmises that the two are praying while the priest is offering up incense.[7]

Josephus (*Antiquities* 17.42) informs us that there were six thousand Pharisees in his day. How he arrived at this figure is unknown. There were two schools of Pharisees: the School of Hillel and the School of Shammai. The former was considered more lenient, the latter stricter. The common people respected and admired the Pharisees as the true interpreters and practitioners of the Old Testament law. Josephus writes of the Pharisees that they "are considered the most accurate interpreters of the laws, and hold the position of the leading sect" (*War* 2.162); and "(they) are extremely influential among the townsfolk; and all prayers and sacred rites of divine worship are performed according to their exposition" (*Antiquities* 18.15).[8]

The Pharisees were the peoples' favorites, as opposed to the Sadducees (only the rich) and the Essenes (the fanatics). The common people celebrated the Pharisees as coming from their ranks. Pharisees were not usually of the wealthy nobility. So, they can't all have been bad. They were the most numerous and most popular sect. The common people trusted them and followed their teaching even if they could not devote the time to become one of them. They would be like—hmm—evangelical Christians today. But is it possible that an evangelical would be that arrogant? Why did Jesus make the Pharisee the example of pride?

In the New Testament Gospels, we even find Pharisees inviting Jesus to dinner (Luke 7:36; 14:1). Pharisees were very careful with whom they ate meals. They regarded many persons as ritually unclean and inappropriate dinner companions. If they ate with Jesus—even invited him to banquets—they were not his enemies. Thus, it seems that Jesus was friends with many of them. In the Gospel of John, one of them, Nicodemus, defends him in the Sanhedrin (John 3:1 and 7:50–51). In one place, several Pharisees warn Jesus to leave the region in which he is ministering because Herod Antipas wants to capture him and kill him as he did John the Baptist (Luke 13:31). They were not all Jesus's enemies.

Do you think Jesus was especially interested in reforming/converting tax collectors? He interacts with and associates with them a lot. He called a tax collector to be one of his close twelve disciples (Matt. 9:9–11). He was considered a "friend of tax collectors" (Matt. 11:19 and Luke 7:34). He shocked people when he announced that tax collectors and prostitutes would enter the kingdom of God ahead of the chief priests and elders (Matt. 21:31). He dined with tax collectors (Luke 15:1, 19:1–10). He seemed to spend a lot of time with both tax collectors and prostitutes. These were the "sinners" of his society. What message would this hold for the modern church?

Tax collectors could become enormously wealthy. One who lived in Caesarea on the coast (named John) once offered the Roman governor a bribe of eight talents of silver (see Chapters Four and Eight for this amount of money). We presume he didn't offer his entire fortune but only a small fraction. Therefore, he must have enjoyed a wealth many times that amount (see Josephus,

War 2.287). How did they become so rich? Often by defrauding and overcharging the common people. Therefore, they were hated.

A bit of cultural information: Kenneth Bailey notes from his decades of living in the Middle East that men almost never beat their chest as the tax collector here does. Women do that in mourning, but men do not. It has to be a very tense and emotional moment for that to happen. This action may tell us how sincere the tax collector was in his repentance.[9]

NOTES

[1] Foster, *Studies in the Life of Christ.*

[2] C. S. Lewis, *Mere Christianity* (New York: MacMillan, 1951).

[3] My paraphrase. More literally, "(A bishop) must not be a recent convert so that he will not become arrogant and fall into the condemnation of the devil." It is possible, however, to interpret this verse as not describing the devil's downfall but the devil's trap, laid for us. Thus, it would read "fall into the condemnation coming from the devil."

[4] There is a famous quotation to that effect in the John Wayne movie, *She Wore a Yellow Ribbon* (1949): "Never apologize; it is a sign of weakness." But the quotation is often repeated in television shows and by politicians. It has become "viral" in our culture.

[5] *Mere Christianity.*

[6] Billy Graham, *World Aflame* (Garden City, NY: Doubleday, 1965), 150–51.

[7] Bailey, *Jesus through Middle Eastern Eyes.*

[8] Translations from the *Loeb Classical Library.*

[9] Bailey, *Jesus through Middle Eastern Eyes.*

7

WHEN YOU CAN FAKE SINCERITY

Matt. 13:24–30 and 37–43

George Burns was a great comedian. He had a joke he told repeatedly throughout his career: "The key to success is sincerity. And when you can fake that, you've got it made." Of course, if you're faking it, you're not really sincere. Kind of funny the way he told it, but not funny in real life. There are too many people just faking it. They don't really care about their customers except for liberating them of some of their cash. They don't really want to serve their constituents; they want the power that comes with the political office. They don't really want to put you in a car that you can rely on; they want to put you in a car that they think you can pay for. On it goes. Too many people are faking it. In the church, we call that "hypocrisy."

There is an old joke about a family that had invited many guests for Sunday dinner. The lady of the house had worked late into Saturday evening and had risen early on Sunday to prepare everything. It was in those old days before air conditioning, and it was going to be a very hot summer day. Finally, church was over, the invited guests—including the minister and his wife—were there, and it was time to eat the feast. The mother and father wanted to show off their piety and asked their young son to offer the blessing for the meal. The little boy was nervous about praying in front of so many people, especially the ministerial couple. He said, "I wouldn't know what to say." The mother whispered to him, "Just say what you've heard me say." She doubtless thought he would repeat one of her pious prayers. But the small boy remembered something more recent. He bowed his little head reverently and exclaimed, "O Lord. Why did I invite all of these people on a hot day like this?" Hypocrisy. Funny under certain circumstances but not funny with respect to serious matters of life.

George Barna and his company do polling—mostly religious polling. A 2018 poll of the Gen Zs (born between 1999 and 2015) revealed that the non-Christian Gen Zs believed that the churches were full of hypocrites and that ministers were very untrustworthy. I doubt that this perception has changed much recently.[1]

More alarming is an essay in *Christianity Today* that reported a waning of ethical integrity in the ministry. Increasingly, ministers are making moral compromises, and others just look the other way.[2] Hypocrisy. Not so funny when it is about serious issues.

In one sense, we are all hypocrites, of course. Even the most ardent sports fan might go for a hot dog while his favorite player bats in the seventh inning. A real fan would skip supper entirely and watch every minute of the game. And a real fan would not talk to others during the game. A real fan would scream support—and, of course, advice—throughout the game. But even the most fanatic follower of a team will not always do that. The same is true of Christians. It is wearying to be always "on" in our religious life. We are only human after all. We grow weak and sometimes let down our guard. We say things we know we shouldn't. We have thoughts we know we shouldn't.

A well-known preacher told a story about himself (I'll mercifully withhold his name) that happened while driving in thick city traffic. Someone cut in front of him suddenly, causing him to have to slam on the brakes to keep from rear-ending the other driver. He reacted angrily by honking his horn. He was still honking as he pulled out to pass the other car. Then he noticed that the driver was one of the elders at the church he served. He said that he immediately changed his facial expression from anger to cheerfulness, pretending to be honking to say hello. Hypocrisy. We are all hypocrites to some extent.

But the hypocrisy Jesus is talking about in this parable is more egregious, much more serious. These people—"weeds"—live a double life. They are like double agents, spies, who present themselves one way in public but have a dark side. They live quite differently in private from what they espouse in public.

I'll never forget the story my father told me about one of the deacons in our church. I was just a boy when my father and one other elder paid the deacon a visit. You see, his wife had been attending church lately with bruises on her arms and face. When that happens once, you can believe that she "fell" down. But when she presents herself in church Sunday after Sunday in such a condition, that should raise suspicions. So, my dad and one other elder visited this man. I'll call him Charles. The elders came right out with it and asked Charles, "Brother, is it possible that you are beating your wife?" I guess Charles erupted with anger. His response was that what he did in his own home was not the church's business. If he wanted to beat his wife daily, he would. He attended church regularly, paid a tithe, and served on the board of deacons. He was a good Christian. His family life was his business. The elders' response was, "No, brother. What you do in your home is also part of the Christian life. You cannot be a deacon and beat your wife. We will move immediately to expel you from the board." Charles was highly insulted and never attended church again. I'm afraid he went to his grave thinking that his Christian life was only what he showed the public and that his private life did not count. Double life. Dark side.

A lady once confessed to me, as she prepared early one morning for surgery. It's usually not a good sign when a surgery patient asks her husband and the attending nurse to step outside so she can talk privately with the minister. She then tearfully confided that she had been sexually abused as a young teenager. She then said that the abuser was now trying to do the same thing to her two young boys. Imagine my shock when she named the abuser: a deacon in a church I was familiar with. Double life; dark side.

I once worked with two men to reconcile their substantial differences. Each had, because of a silly dispute, said more than he should and the disagreement had gotten out of hand. In those situations, you want to gently nudge Christian brothers to forgive and move on. But in the process of my counseling, one of the brothers said to the other, "I've hated you for a long time." Wow! I did not see that one coming. How can you call yourself a Christian, worship alongside a brother for decades, and then say that? Double life; dark side.

I remember a very famous "evangelist" and college president from several decades back. He was a rising star in the conservative movement in the church and in politics. He had a sort of crusade to save America from communism. I heard him speak in person once and found his delivery electrifying. He had the talent to go far. He had already risen rather far. Then, it came out that he was sexually molesting the young people in his college (of both sexes). The revelation came when a newly married couple confessed to each other, on their wedding night, that this creep had molested them both. Double life; dark side.

Recently (June 2019), the leader of a mega-megachurch, with more than one million members worldwide, was indicted on twenty-six felony counts for child rape, child pornography, and sex trafficking. He was arrested along with two female members of his church who assisted him in his evil.[3] Imagine that! The spiritual leader of a million Christian brothers and sisters, the ambassador for Christ on this earth, was abusing little children and women! Darkness. Weeds.

It boggles the mind to understand the depth of that dark hypocrisy. Weeds! They will be ripped up at the Day of Judgment, but for now, they often grow among the wheat and we do not know the difference—until something like this happens and we realize that the weeds are still with us.

In the parable, the sower is Christ, the good seed (wheat) represents the sincere members of the kingdom, the enemy who sows the weeds is the devil, the weeds are the egregious hypocrites, and the harvest is the judgment day. How many of our Christian heroes will be called out on that day as weeds? *No matter how acclaimed you may be now, you can't hide on the Day of Judgment.*

The hypocrites that Jesus is talking about in this parable, the weeds, believe that they are rather entitled to their two lives. They want the acclaim of being a good Christian—that's why they pretend to be wheat—but also the freedom to abuse, to hurt, to violate, and to sin at will. They love their public persona. They develop it carefully. But they also believe that they have a right to a private one, one of their own choosing. They are special. Ordinary moral standards do not apply to them. Double life; dark side.

The problem is that the hypocrites, instead of repenting of sin, only regret getting caught. They mourn the humiliation, not the trespass. Sure, it is embarrassing to be caught in some action that totally belies everything you have allegedly stood for. But why were you not ashamed of your behavior before you were caught?

A major problem in many church denominations—including mine—is that we do not teach about repentance. We seem to focus on the show. We want to hold up as models those that do great things or have great talents. But teaching about the heart, about sincere devotion, and repentance for wrong is often lacking. It does not sell well in our society. But it "sells" with God. Repentance is the antidote to hypocrisy.

Notice in the parable, the laborers (angels) want to pull up the weeds from the good plants. But the master (God) will not allow it. In Israel, it is very hard to distinguish a certain kind of weed from wheat in its early stage of growth. At harvest, it is much easier to tell which is the wheat. The weeds or darnel produce black grain, but the wheat produces white grain. Others think the problem is that the roots of the weeds are intertwined with the roots of the good wheat. If you pull one up, you might pull up the other. Whatever the case is, it is a problem to just rip out the weeds now. So, the workers/angels wait. All will be revealed at the harvest/judgment day. At the moment, the weeds think they are fooling the people of God.

It is sometimes really difficult for us to tell what is in a person's heart. We see actions that look suspicious, but we find out later that they were not. But if we form hardened opinions based on our hasty observations, then we may have a false view of that person for many years. Let me give a personal (and humorous) example. My mother lived for a while in an assisted living institution. Most of the residents could no longer drive a car, and many of them, as was common in their generation (and in Eastern Kentucky), smoked. So, whenever I came for a visit, several of them would give me money and ask me to buy their cigarettes for them. One day I was leaving a convenience store with an armload of several cartons of cigarettes when I encountered a lady who worked at the Christian university where I was employed. At this university, the use of tobacco was strictly prohibited for all employees. She looked at what I was carrying, gasped, and offered a weak "Hello." I thought to myself, "To explain would be fruitless. I'll just pretend everything is perfectly normal." So, I offered a cheerful greeting and continued to my car. I never did explain to her what I was doing. It was an act of kindness but could have been interpreted as an act of defiance of the rules of my employer. It is sometimes difficult to tell the weeds from the wheat.

Jesus taught that judgment was an act that only God should do and in his own time. Meanwhile, we live among the weeds, sometimes not knowing for certain who the weeds are and who the wheat is, and we allow God alone to judge. Jesus was teaching both that there will be a Day of Judgment and that in the meantime we should not be sectarian—habitually excommunicating sinners and shunning those we do not think are living up to our standards. We must avoid attempts to remove ourselves radically from our world by living in a closed community and keeping out non-Christians or weak Christians. We should, rather, be a light in the world. Don't try to root out the weeds; you might throw out some wheat at the same time.

Jim Bakker was a famous television evangelist in the seventies. He was climbing high and raising tons of money. He lived a life of luxury, with large mansions and luxury automobiles. He taught and lived the health and wealth gospel: that God wants you to be rich and never become sick. Then, his life crashed and burned. He was arrested, tried, and sentenced to many years in prison for fraud. After prison, he sought to restore his ministry. He wrote a book entitled *I Was Wrong*. In the book, he confesses that he had misunderstood both the Bible and the Christian faith. His adherence to the prosperity gospel was heresy; it was wrong. He admits that his behavior was sinful and self-centered. He writes, "I did not understand what it means to let Jesus be the Lord of my life."

Now not many of us will write a book confessing our sin, but all of us need to have this attitude about it. We all need to believe and confess to God that we are selfish, that we often behave in a self-centered manner, ignoring the needs and hurts of others, and that we often "use" our faith for ourselves, not in gratitude to a gracious God. It is very easy to enjoy the acclaim of being a dedicated Christian—especially when we are with our Christian friends—but not actually be interested in being one.

So, we face up to our secret sins, we repent sincerely, and we ask for forgiveness and transformation. We stop living a double life and close down those parts that dishonor God and harm others. Further, we refrain from judging since we often make mistakes and since God is the ultimate judge.

All of us need regular self-examinations of our soul. Are we living a double life? Is God the lord of our private life as well as our public life? We can fool others, but we cannot fool God. We can't fake sincerity with him. The words of 1 John 1:9 are important: "If we confess our sins, he is faithful and just and will forgive us."

DISCUSSION QUESTIONS

1. How do you think people who live a double life justify it to themselves?

2. Why do you think we need to be cautious about judging who are the "weeds" of our church?

3. Does your church stress the role of repentance enough in your opinion?

4. This is one of the only two parables for which Jesus himself gave the interpretation. (The other one is the Parable of the Four Soils. See Chapter Five.) Why do you think Jesus deemed it necessary to give the interpretation of this parable?

GOING DEEPER

When they planted seeds in those days, they simply scattered them on the ground and came back later to plow them under (see Chapter Five). They did not use rows and furrows. Thus, you could not tell which was the wheat by what was in line with the row.

The act of planting weeds in another family's wheat field did happen from time to time, apparently. One New Testament scholar, who had grown up in Palestine in the 1920s, reported a similar incident among Arab farmers in his day.[4] This would be one way to harm your enemy and his family, anonymously.

Does it seem unbelievable that some "enemy" would spoil your crops of wheat in this cruel manner? Malina and Rohrbaugh explain: "Feuding families and feuding groups marked the social landscape of the first-century Mediterranean world. Being born into a given family, a person normally inherited a ready-made set of friends and enemies."[5] In other words, what Jesus was using as background for his story was a common phenomenon in first-century Palestinian society.

The weeds or tares were a common headache to the Palestinian farmer. The rabbinic literature speaks frequently of wheat fields being spoiled by tares. The Mishnah declares, "Wheat and tares do not qualify as mixed crops" (m. Kilaim 1:1). They mean having tares mixed in with wheat is so common that it does not invalidate the crop (see Lev. 19:9 and Deut. 22:6–11 on mixed crops). In one rabbinic midrash it says, "Everything has since the Flood corrupted its way . . . People plant wheat and get tares . . ." (Gen. R. 28). In another place it tells a story in which "every threshing floor is covered with tares . . ." (Num. R. 4).[6] These references establish that weeds or tares spoiling the wheat was a serious problem in ancient Palestine in the time of Jesus. Jesus used a very common plight to illustrate his teaching.

I have interpreted the parable as an exposé on the hypocrisy within the church, but the text (vv. 38 and 41) says that the parable refers to the world and the kingdom of God within the world. Blomberg explains: "The kingdom in verse 41 . . . must refer to God's universal, sovereign reign rather than being equated with the church."[7] The kingdom is God's reign on this earth, which is broader and older than the church itself, as well as eternal. But as an earthly and present group devoted to God's reign, the church also fits this parable. God's reign in this world—of which the church is a part—has those who sincerely believe in it and those who only fake it.

NOTES

[1] "Gen Z: Your Questions Answered," Barna, February 6, 2018, www.barna.com/research/gen-z-questions-answered/.

[2] David Augsburger, "The Private Lives of Public Leaders," *Christianity Today*, December 11, 2006, www.christianitytoday.com/ct/2006/decemberweb-only/private-lives-public-leaders-integrity.html.

[3] "Bail Set at $50M for La Luz Del Mundo Church Leader Accused of Child Rape, Sex Trafficking," *CBS News Los Angeles*, June 6, 2019, https://losangeles.cbslocal.com/2019/06/06/bail-set-at-50m-for-la-luz-del-mundo-church-leader-accused-of-child-rape-sex-trafficking/.

[4] Joachim Jeremias, *The Parables of Jesus* (New York: Charles Scribner's Sons, 1963).

[5] Malina and Rohrbaugh, *Social-Science Commentary.*

[6] Translations in Strack and Billerbeck, *Kommentar.*

[7] Craig L. Blomberg, *Interpreting the Parables* (Downers Grove, IL: InterVarsity Press, 1990).

8

AMERICA'S GOT TALENTS

Matt. 25:14–30

I heard about a guy whose boss was a real tyrant. He was very demanding. He often gave his employee extra work to do only minutes before quitting time and expected the report or proposal to be ready by 8:00 A.M. the next morning. Heaven help the employee if it was not ready on time. The boss would unleash a torrent of verbal abuse and threats. The employee lived in fear of the boss. He knew the boss could fire him at any minute over the slightest offense, real or imagined.

Then the boss met an early demise (angry people usually do not live a long life). The next boss was as different as night from day. He was kind and considerate. When the employee's wife became gravely ill, the new boss was very concerned and solicitous of her well-being. The new boss gave small presents to the employee's children on occasion. If there was an extra job to do—the report or proposal—the boss stayed with the employee to help get it done and paid the employee overtime. Pretty soon the employee realized something: he loved his job. He was working as hard as he had under the old boss but he loved his work now because he loved his new boss.

That's what this parable is about: get out and work your best for the kingdom because you love God.

A man, obviously a wealthy man with many business concerns, was preparing to take a long journey. He called three of his top servants for a meeting and assigned each of them a portion of the business. He gave one man five talents (see Chapter Four) to work with, gave another two talents, and the third received one talent. In the parable, Jesus says he gave to each according to his ability. Then he went away, and after a long while, returned and demanded an account of what they had done. While he had been away, the five-talent man had doubled his money; the two-talent man had also doubled his money. But the one-talent man had done nothing. The master was happy with the first two servants but very angry with the third. In the parable, the "talents" (really a weight of silver coins) represent the "resources" and "gifts" God has given us for service.[1]

The five-talent man was obviously very skilled at business. He was one of those superstars who are able to turn any project into gold. And given the chance, he used his extraordinary gifts to bear fruit. We should thank God for such people when they use their gifts for him. We all know a few of these: They are the megachurch pastors who lead a small congregation of a hundred people to a super congregation of tens of thousands. They are the missionaries who settle in a foreign land and establish thousands of schools and medical clinics leading to tens of thousands of converts. They are wealthy and successful businesspersons who use their fabulous wealth for God, giving enormous sums to missions and charities.

They are sports superstars who give a witness for Christ, leveraging their fame and status for an opportunity to witness both by word and by example. They are musicians who win Grammys for their Christian music. We are impressed and thankful for such persons. They are the five-talent servants.

To this servant the master was effusive with praise: "Well done, you good and faithful servant!" The master was delighted with the success and immediately gave the five-talent man more responsibility, and with it, undoubtedly, more acclaim.

Of course, we do not know what happened next in this servant's life. Upon his enormous success and reward, did he become conceited? Did he lapse? Did he get involved in a suicidal lifestyle of drugs and alcohol? It often happens with superstars. Superstars often fail to realize two things: Their talent is a gift from God. They did not earn it; they only developed it. If someone can slam-dunk a basketball, he or she started out with a certain amount of physical giftedness that cannot be taught or acquired. If someone can sing like an opera star, he or she was born with the gift. Five-talent servants should accept that their extraordinary gifts are just that: gifts. They are no better than anybody else, because they did not earn their gifts; they were born with them.

Additionally, superstars should also allow for being in the right place at the right time. A newspaper reporter once asked a successful farmer how he explained his success. The farmer replied, "Well, 50 percent is weather, 50 percent is luck, and the rest is my fantastic intelligence." That farmer knew the truth: many five-talent persons were just in the right place at the right time. Megachurches don't grow everywhere. Not all foreign missions have the kind of success that was described above. If the same missionary went to a different country, he or she might have much more modest success. Many talented athletes never make it to the "big leagues" because they are injured. Many very talented singers are never given a shot at fame and stardom. If you are a five-talent person, always consider that, but for the grace of God—not only in the original gift but also in placing you in the right position—you could just as easily have been a two- or one-talent person.

Then to the second servant, the master gave two talents. Notice what the second servant did *not* do: He did not complain that he had been given only two talents and not five. He did not become jealous. If you are a two-talent man or woman, relax. So are 99 percent of the rest of humanity. So, you're not in the top 1 percent; so what? Get over it and be what God has made you. Very few Christian pastors will lead a megachurch. Very few missionaries will have the kind of phenomenal success described above. Few can earn billions in order to give it away. Few will win a Grammy or a Heisman Trophy. Most of us will minister at medium to small churches, will serve in foreign missions which see a modest number of converts, and will sing a little in church but never become famous. Or maybe your gift is visiting the sick, working in vacation Bible school, or comforting the grieving. You will never win the Nobel Peace Prize for it, will not become famous for it, but you do your best. You are a two-talent Christian. Hooray for you! So are the vast majority of your brothers and sisters.

So, what did the master say to the two-talent man? Did he say, "Not too bad a job, you fairly good and fairly faithful servant?" No, he said the exact words he had just delivered to the five-talent man: "Well done, you good and faithful servant!" The master did not care how much money they made for him (i.e., how successful they were in the world's eyes). He cared how faithful each person was. The master did not expect more from the two-talent man than he was capable of doing.

I read a story about a guy who lives in Michigan. He owns a car repair shop, but much of his business comes from plowing out snow in winter. In 2007 there was more snow than usual, even for

Michigan. It was time to make some big money. At the same time, he heard that food pantries around the county were running out of food. So, he had an idea. When he plowed someone's driveway or street, he asked for only partial payment and took the rest in a sack of nonperishable food items. Soon the cab of his truck was full of food, and he took it to his church's food pantry. Then other snowplow operators heard about his plan and they began to participate. Eventually, the food pantries all around the region were full.[2] This was a two-talent guy whose resource was his snowplow. But he used it. Jesus would have said to him, "Well done."

As I write this, the world is rocked by the terrible coronavirus pandemic of 2020. Each day more cases are confirmed and more and more die. People are scared. Millions are out of work. But in the middle of all this chaos, you have to be impressed by how some persons have reached out to help. The following was tweeted on April 3, 2020:

> God bless the maintenance man at the Motel 6 who noticed the homeless family living in room 203 and brought them food from home. May the bread he's broken in order to share with them multiply to feed each hungry mouth. Amen.[3]

Here's a guy who worked in maintenance at an inexpensive motel. He may have considered himself a one-talent man. He can't have had, I would think, an abundance of food at home for his family. But he did what he could, and he was a hero. Jesus would say to him, "Well done."

Then there was the one-talent man. This guy did nothing. He says he was afraid of losing the money, and so he buried it. But the master calls him lazy. The one-talent guy just did not want to serve. Notice his three misconceptions: First, he had a false conception of God. He thought of God as harsh and cruel (v. 24). Second, he thought the Christian life was just a matter of not doing anything wrong. His thinking was, don't mess up, don't lose anything. This is like the Christian who thinks Christian ethics is obeying all the prohibitions of the Bible, keeping all the "thou-shalt-nots." But Christian ethics is loving God with all your being and your neighbor as yourself. Those are not prohibitions; they are positive motivations to do something. Third, the one-talent man was motivated by fear (v. 25). This is like the Christian who fails to see God as a God of grace and mercy, a God who loves. And so, he just played a kind of preventive defense. He said to himself, "Just don't make a mistake; don't mess up, because God is just waiting to strike you with a lightning bolt when you do."

Faith without works is like a bird without wings. You will never soar to the heights of Christian joy and Christian experience without an effort. The Christian life is not just obeying the prohibitions.

After John Wilkes Booth shot President Lincoln in the back of the head, he jumped over the balcony of Ford's Theater and onto the stage. Then he exited out the back door to a waiting horse. He rode south into Virginia, pursued by the Union Army. Eventually, they found him and surrounded him in a barn. Although they intended to take him alive for trial, a soldier, inserting his rifle between the boards of the barn, became trigger-happy and shot him in the neck. They dragged Booth out of the barn badly wounded. He was evidently paralyzed from the neck down. He asked to see his hands, perhaps because he had no feeling in them. They held his hands up for him. He looked at them and said, "Useless." Those were his last words.

Don't let that be the characterization of your life: "Useless." Get up, get out, and do something. If you make a mistake, so what? We all do. Just do something. Use your two talents—or for some of you, your five talents—to the glory of God and for the edification of the church.

A well-known preacher found himself sitting beside an NFL head coach on a plane. The preacher tried to strike up a casual conversation. He asked the coach how his team was looking for the new season. The coach responded enthusiastically that he was optimistic because he had so much talent on the team. That piqued the interest of the preacher. He asked, "What's talent?" He wanted to know how this guy who was getting paid to assess athletes defined talent. The answer was a surprise.

The NFL head coach thought for a while and then answered, "The drive to win is the talent."[4] At the end of the day, we all have certain gifts, but those who contribute the most (to the team, to their constituents, to their company—to the kingdom of God) *want* to do so.

These are two-talent women and men because of what they *are*, not because of the gifts they have. Be that; *want* to make a difference and you will.

DISCUSSION QUESTIONS

1. Do you ever find yourself feeling jealous of those receiving more acclaim than you for their Christian work?

2. Do you have trouble figuring out what your talent is? Have you helped somebody else discover his or her gifts?

3. Do you think most Christians are motivated by love of God or by fear of God in their service?

4. Do you think that this parable could be used abusively to make those contributing modestly to the kingdom feel inferior or bad about themselves?

GOING DEEPER

The term translated "talent" comes from a Greek word that sounds a lot like our English word but doesn't mean the same thing at all. It refers to a weight of money. It equals about sixty-six pounds of silver coins or around six thousand[5] silver denarii (see Chapter Four). If one assumes, as most do, that the average daily wage of a day laborer was one denarius (see Chapter Three), a talent equaled six thousand days of labor. In that case—calculating based on the US federal minimum wage—one talent of silver denarii equals around $348,000. The five talents the first servant received would equal $1,740,000.

When the one-talent man buried his money in the ground, he behaved the way most poor persons in this time did. The rabbis said: "A poor person digs a hole to hide his coins" (b. Shabbat 102b); "There is only one place to store money securely: in the ground" (b. Baba Metzia 42a).[6] But they also would sometimes hide their money in the ceiling or in the walls of their house. The one-talent man was not thinking about how he could use the money the master left with him. He wanted to store it. He was afraid of losing it. But Jesus's point in the parable is that you also lose it if you don't use it.

The practice of a master giving servants resources to use for him is found in a few rabbinic parables. In the one below, we can see the same principle at work that is in Jesus's parable:

> A mortal king . . . had two servants whom he loved with utter love. To one he gave a measure of wheat and to the other he gave a measure of wheat, to one a bundle of flax and to the other a bundle of flax. What did the clever one of the two do? He took the flax and wove it into a table cloth. He took the wheat and made it into fine flour by sifting the grain first and grinding it. Then he kneaded the dough and baked it, set the loaf upon the table, spread the tablecloth over it, and kept it to await the coming of the king. But the foolish one of the two did not do anything at all. After a while, the king came into the house and said to the two servants, "My sons, bring me what I gave you." One brought out the table with [the loaf baked of] fine flour on it, and with the tablecloth spread over it. And the other brought out his wheat in a basket with the bundle of flax over the wheat grains. What a shame! What a disgrace! Need it be asked which of the two servants was the more beloved? He, of course, who laid out the table with [the loaf baked of] fine flour upon it.[7]

The parable has many of the same elements as Jesus's parable. A master gives servants resources and expects them to use them advantageously. In this rabbinic parable, however, each servant receives the same amount of resources (as in the Luke 19:12–27 Parable of the Pounds/Minas). There are only two servants in the rabbinic parable instead of the three in Matthew. But in both the master returns and demands an accounting. Placing Jesus's parable alongside this rabbinic one helps us to interpret his parable more clearly. First, both parables say do your best with what God has given you. We can all contribute in some small way. Second, in the rabbinic parable, the master loves the industrious servant more than the lazy one. Jesus does not say that. He simply condemns the laziness of the third servant. I think it would be a mistake to think we are making God love us more or earning extra "stars in our crown" in heaven by doing good deeds, by using our talents. You're not making God love you more. God can't love you more than he already does. If God loved the fallen and evil world so much he gave his son (John 3:16), how could he love you any more? But God does expect us to contribute in some way to his kingdom. So, the second way this rabbinic parable clarifies Jesus's parable for us is by way of contrast.

NOTES

[1] Blomberg, *Parables.*

[2] Dave Browning, "Making a Difference at Christmas," in *A Cool Drink of Water* (New York: Guideposts, 2010), 144–46.

[3] Tweeted by Jonathan Wilson-Hartgrove (@wilsonhartgrove, April 3, 2020).

[4] Robert H. Schuller, *Reach Out for New Life* (Garden Grove, CA: Cathedral Press, 1977).

[5] Danker, *Greek-English Lexicon.*

[6] See Strack and Billerbeck, *Kommentar.*

[7] Quoted in Robert Doran, "The Parable of the Talents/Pounds: Apocalyptic Warning or Economic Critique?" *Biblica* 100/4 (2019): 527–42. Text from W. G. Braude and I. J. Kapstein, *Tanna debē Eliyyahu* (Philadelphia: Jewish Publication Society, 1981).

9

THE BORROWED SOUL

Luke 12:15–21

I met a man a few years ago who was then in his mideighties. He had amassed thousands of acres of farmland during his lifetime. When I met him, he was trying to buy yet another small farm. He was pushy and aggressive, trying to bully a family into selling him their inheritance at his price. The price wasn't a bad one but wasn't the best offer. He insisted that he ought to have the first right to buy the farm because he owned all the other farms on that highway. As a matter of fact, he already owned most of the farmland in the area. He acted angry that the family balked at selling him their farm, their family's inheritance, the little piece of ground that had been the livelihood for the family for so long. To them, it was part of the family; to the large landowner, it was just another acquisition. It wasn't that he needed more land to support himself or his business. It wasn't even that he just wanted to be the biggest farmer in the region. It wasn't about competition or having more than anybody else. He wanted *all* the land. He owned every piece of land along the highway except this one. He had to have it all. Well, the family ended up selling the land to someone else, and the angry octogenarian land-buyer passed away a year or so later.

I often asked myself why this guy thought he had to have that piece of land. What was going on there? He already had several times more land that he needed to live like a millionaire. He was, I would guess, at age eighty-five, sort of retired. What was happening? I concluded, perhaps ungenerously, that the guy just was greedy.

Greed is not about having enough; it's not even about having more than someone else (competitiveness; see Chapter Six). Greed is about having it all. That's why Jesus warns in this parable, "Guard against greed, because a person's life is not (given meaning) by having a lot of wealth" (v. 15). Then Jesus goes further by telling the parable of verses 16–20 to illustrate his point. In the story, a guy's fields yield a bumper crop. He has never seen such produce in his life. He has nowhere to put it all. Notice he does not think about giving some of it to the poor. He reflects on it and finally has a solution. He enters into a massive building program. He constructs huge granaries. Then he stores up all the grain in his colossal new barns, assuming he will have many years of the lifestyle of the rich and famous. But no sooner is this project all finished than he dies. He stored up all that wealth[1] for nothing.

But the point of the story is not that you shouldn't plan for the future because life is fragile and full of ups and downs; the point is a little different and is based on a certain word in verse 20. This word makes it clear that all we possess, we have on loan from God. Someday, we must give it back. The one Greek word translated "will be demanded from you" (NIV), "is required of you" (NASB), or "is being demanded of you" (NRSV) is the term they used to refer to payment for something or repayment of a loan. It's what you owe and must be paid or paid back.

The first problem with this Rich Fool (as most commentaries call him) is that he does not appreciate that all we have is from God.[2] That means everything. You didn't choose your parents, your DNA, your place of birth, and the environment in which you grew up. That means that if you are attractive, you have nothing to brag about. You didn't do it; it was just there. If you are not considered by some to be attractive, you have no reason to feel ashamed; you just inherited it. Even if you worked hard, created a business, and succeeded, you have nothing to brag about. Who gave you that drive, that determination? You got that from God as well. If you worked two jobs while earning straight A's in college and graduated to an exciting career, again, you inherited the drive and the intelligence to do all that. Don't think you're special. Jesus's point is, it's all a loaner. You'll have to pay it back someday.

I'll never forget the first house loan my wife and I received. It was pretty scary to sign our names to such a large sum of money for so long a time. It was nice to live in the house, but daunting to think that we owed that much money. When you borrow things, people expect to be paid back. There is a reckoning out there in the future. The Rich Fool did not expect he owed anything. He thought it all belonged to him. He had prospered because he was special. No, sorry. It was a loaner. There aren't really any self-made women or men. We are all God-made. The problem is, many don't know it.

Think about what God has loaned us: Our children are not really ours, are they? We raise them, love them, invest ourselves in them, but they do not really "belong" to us. If you think that way, you need to think again. They are not your property. Our job or career is not really ours. Someday we will have to give it up either in retirement or loss. Our spouse is not "ours" in the sense of ownership. Even our bank account is not actually ours. Somebody else will get it someday. We are just a caretaker of it. It all has to be "paid back" in a sense.

But the real shocker in this parable is that even our life is on loan. "This night your life must be paid back" (verse 20).[3] We even have a borrowed life! Here we have an interesting play on words. The word translated first "self" and then "life" in the NIV, "soul" in NASB (both times), and first "soul" and then "life" in the NRSV translations is the Greek word *psychē*. This term can mean "life," "inner person," or "self."

Table 9.1: Translations of *Psychē* (Life, Inner Person, Self)

	NIV	NASB	NRSV
Verse 19	-self	soul	soul
Verse 20	life	soul	life

So, Jesus has a play on words in verses 19 and 20: "I will say to my *psychē*, 'Hey, *Psychē!* You've got millions stashed away. Yippee! Kick back; put on the feedbag; hoist a few; party hearty.' But God said to him, 'Fool, tonight I'm calling in the loan of your *psychē*.'"[4]

All we have is from God. Let that sink into your *psychē*.

The second problem with the "Rich Fool" mentality is that when we ignore that all we have is from God, we get into protectionism and selfishness. Notice how often this guy refers to himself. He talks about *his* goods, *his* barns, *his* crops, *his* grain, and *his psychē*. He further thinks the expected rest is his, the upcoming food is his, the looked-for drink is his, and the parties out there in the future are his (verse 19). It's all his—in his mind—and nobody else's.[5]

My youthful athletic career was unimpressive. Oh, I dreamed about pitching for the Yankees someday, even though I played second base and had never pitched a game in my life. But that's the way it goes for children. You can learn a lot about life, however, playing sports. I remember I was playing second base in a night game in high school. Someone hit a pop fly which was really right to me. But the center fielder—the "hotdogger" on the team—started calling from way out in center field, "Mine! Mine! Mine!" I couldn't believe it. But the rule is, infielders yield to outfielders on fly balls. So, I took one step to my left and waited. The ball would have literally hit me in the head had I not moved. The hotdog rushed in from center field and arrived just in time to have the ball hit his glove and bounce out. Mr. "Mine! Mine!" should have yelled "Not mine! Not mine!"

Well, I guess we all should. We all should have that attitude about all our blessings. They are not ours; God has loaned them to us. My money is "Not mine!" My house is "Not mine!" My talents are "Not mine!" And my life is "Not mine!" Oh, I intend to take care of all these things. I want to use them for the glory of God, but they are not really mine.

The Rich Fool failed to appreciate that God had anything to do with it. It is idolatrous and ungrateful to leave God out of your thinking in this way. We need to remember this when we speak of "my kids, my money, my spouse, my career, my abilities—my life." These are items God has given you. Take care of them; use them wisely and reverently. Treat them with love, giving thanks regularly to God.

I'll never forget my counseling with a wealthy couple. I'll call them the Smiths. I arrived at the Smiths' house and was immediately shown around their expansive estate. The house was not only large but had very expensive items in it. Then they took me to their buildings outside the house to show me their boat and million-dollar motor home. We finally sat down in their living room, and they informed me about how much money they had made in the last ten years (each year was more than I will make in a lifetime). They were nice people, but the conversation always focused on what they owned. And they "owned" a lot.

Finally, we sort of got down to business. You see, I had come because the Smiths had been attending the church where I preached. They were interested in becoming Christians. They wanted to know what that involved. Now I didn't say they had to get down in the pigpen and ask God to have mercy (see Chapter Six), as the servant had advised the rich man in the Middle Ages. I just talked about committing your life—and possessions—to Jesus Christ as the lord of your life. I don't think I laid it on too heavily. I just talked to them as I would anyone inquiring about what it means to be a Christian. But at the end of the conversation, they seemed sort of scared off. They said something like, "I guess there's a lot more to it than we thought." This was not going to be like joining a club. This endeavor was a whole new way of thinking and living. They ultimately said they would think about it. They never became Christians as far as I knew. It is difficult for all of us to accept that it does not belong to us; not our money, not our house, not our boat, not our motor home, not our furnishings—not our life.

Whenever I hear someone say, "It's my life, I'll do as I please," I cringe. Aren't these words echoing the Rich Fool? I once saw a teenager wearing a T-shirt that said, "I'm not here for a long time. I'm here for a good time." Yikes!

The third issue that arises from the Rich Fool mentality is the failure to think about payback. This is a big problem. Notice the text in verse 20 does not say, "Tonight, your life will end," or "Tonight, your life is over." Rather it says, "Tonight you have to pay back the loan of your life (*psychē*)." Your debt has been called in. Just as we have to pay back our house loan, so we have to "pay back" the loan of our life. It never was ours; it always was a loaner. We don't so much give it up as pay it back to the God who graciously loaned it to us for a little while.

In other words, there is a judgment, a reckoning, an accounting coming. The metaphor of paying back the loan is another way of saying that there will be a judgment day. On that day, we will have to explain how we used the loan of our life. It is not "our life"; it never was. That's why Jesus concludes, "Who's now going to get what you acquired in life?" (verse 20b). God will now loan it to someone else.

Let's say you loaned someone your new car. In three weeks, he or she brings it back. It has a smashed-in front fender, numerous dings on the doors, and paint missing on the hood. The interior of the car has been trashed. It looks like an old junk heap now. What would you ask the borrower? "What have you been doing with the car I loaned you?" Someday God will ask us what we have done with the life he loaned us.

As I write this, the coronavirus is attacking the planet. Not only are many dying, but more and more are out of work and very fearful about their economic future. These are very insecure times. Interestingly, this is also Holy Week, the days between Palm Sunday and Easter. During this week, we should be particularly vigilant about spiritual matters. I don't know. Maybe it takes a worldwide pandemic to press us to do that. But this situation has taught us how quickly our security, our self-confidence, and our prosperity can go away. We had built bigger barns, and they have collapsed. We are made aware—if we really do *Hear Now*—that it all was a loaner. How will you think about your life now that the world has suffered this attack?

DISCUSSION QUESTIONS

1. Do you think greed is a problem in our society today?

2. Have you known any persons like the Rich Fool?

3. How do you adjust your thinking about earthly life when you think of it as a loaner?

4. Now that we have learned a little about the flexible word *psychē*, how do you interpret the following verses? "What does it profit a man if he gains the whole world but loses his *psychē*?" (Mark 8:36). "What could a person give in exchange for his *psychē*?" (Mark 8:37).

GOING DEEPER

The word *psychē* can mean (1) life on earth, the breath of life, or life principle; (2) the seat and center of inner human life (center of emotions and feelings); (3) the self.[6] In this parable, Jesus uses meaning (1) in verse 20 and meaning (3) in verse 19. That is why this same word is translated in different ways in the NIV ("self" in v. 19 and "life" in v. 20), as "soul" and "life" in the NRSV, and consistently as "soul" in the NASB in these verses. It does not mean "soul" in the sense of the eternal part of human beings.

The Greek word *paraiteō* means "demand something back as due" (either of a loan or stolen property). This is the word used in verse 20 and translated "will be demanded."[7]

The ancients were especially resentful of hoarders. Those who hoarded grain in giant storehouses and then refused to share in times of famine were considered very evil persons. The insatiably greedy rich persons were seen as especially evil since the ancients believed in a "limited good." That is, they believed that the economic pie was limited. There were only so many pieces, and if someone—some rich family—took too many pieces, that did not leave enough for the rest. Anyone with surplus ought to feel ashamed if he or she did not share with the poor. Of course, our man in the parable never gave the poor a thought.[8]

There were well-known persons who had large granaries for their private use. Berenice, great-granddaughter of Herod the Great, owned a huge barn or granary in the plain south of Galilee.[9] Jesus may have fashioned part of his parable around having seen this granary at some point. He certainly traveled in the great plain south of Nazareth (Luke 7:11). But hers can't have been the only such facility.

The story of a rich man hoarding goods and then retiring to live high only to die immediately thereafter must have been common. There is a reference to this common event in the apocryphal text called The Wisdom of Jesus ben Sirah. This text, written around 180 BC by a Jerusalem sage, describes a man acquiring great wealth through hard work and through depriving himself of things for many years. But now he has made his fortune, many times over, and is ready to kick back, like our man in the parable, and enjoy one big party. But what does he find? "He says, 'I have found rest. Now I will banquet from my (stored-up) goods.' But he doesn't know when the time is coming in which he must leave all of it to somebody else and die"[10] (11:19). The moral lesson in Ben Sirah is that you think you have it all under control but you don't. You worked for this moment, but this moment was taken from you.

Obviously, this moment of feasting is not what you should invest your life in. What is the moral lesson of Jesus's parable?

NOTES

[1] In the ancient world, food was wealth.

[2] Foster, *Studies in the Life of Christ*: "He imagined that he was a 'self-made man.'"

[3] As Jeremias, *Parables,* writes: "Life is a loan. God gave it, and declares that its return will be demanded."

[4] My paraphrase.

[5] As Bailey, *Poet and Peasant and through Peasant Eyes,* writes: "The Rich Fool can only talk to himself. His only audience is his own soul. He, sadly, has no one else around him."

[6] Danker, *Greek-English Lexicon.* The Hebrew word *nephesh* is used about the same way as the Greek word *psyche*: "Bless the Lord, O my *nephesh*" (Ps. 103:1).

[7] Danker, *Greek-English Lexicon.*

[8] See Malina and Rohrbaugh, *Social-Science Commentary.*

[9] Josephus, *Life* 119. Josephus saw the granary during the Jewish War of AD 66–73, decades after Jesus's ministry. But such granaries surely had existed for some time. It is likely that Berenice inherited the granary from her wealthy family.

[10] Translated from the Greek LXX text.

10

BUDDY, CAN YOU SPARE A DIME?

Luke 16:19–31

You may have seen that photograph of a running shoe online. To some, the shoe appears to be pink with white trim, and to others, it appears to be gray with blue-green trim.[1] Does this difference in perception mean anything? Probably not, though some maintained that it meant you were either left-brained (gray and blue-green) or right-brained (pink and white). The photo is interesting because people are sure the colors appear to everyone the way they appear to them. They can't understand how anybody could see colors other than the ones they see. For me, the phenomenon points out a spiritual truth: the spiritual view reality in a different way than the unspiritual.

What is the parable of the Rich Man and Lazarus about? Many have insisted through the years that the story is a sort of video of what is going on in hell and heaven right now. "If you want to know what your deceased friends and relatives are doing at the moment, read this parable" has often been the advice. But I don't think this is the main point here. The main point is, what do you see? When you look at the wealthy and famous of the world and then at the poor and outcasts, what do you see? What you see might not be what others see.

How do you look at reality? Had you been alive in Jesus's day, how would you have viewed the rich man and Lazarus? To help us understand, we might try to contemporize the story. The rich man today lives in a multimillion-dollar condominium in New York City. Lazarus today lives and sleeps on the sidewalk in front of the condo. The rich man wears the finest clothes: his suits are from Alexander Amosu; his workout shoes are Air Jordan Silver. Lazarus wears filthy and smelly rags he found thrown out behind Goodwill. The rich man dines at the most expensive and exclusive restaurants in Manhattan. Lazarus dumpster-dives in the alleys behind those restaurants for his meals. The rich man is in the pink of health: he works out three times a week at his club, he is tanned, and he has the best medical care money can buy. Lazarus is sick with a horrible disease that has left his entire body covered with painful, oozing boils. His medical plan? He lets dogs lick his sores.

Although Lazarus sleeps on the sidewalk in front of the rich man's condo, the rich man never notices Lazarus, even as he sometimes steps over him to walk to his limousine. We tend to screen out poverty from our consciousness.

If you were an observer of those two human beings, what would you see? Most people in Jesus's day observed the rich man and saw success, a winner. They longed to be like him. But Jesus looked at him and saw flames. Most people looked at poor Lazarus and saw a loser—if, indeed, they looked in his direction at all. Jesus looked at him and saw blessedness: "Blessed are the poor" (Luke 6:20).

We should not think Jesus was condemning wealth per se and promising salvation and blessedness to poverty per se. Just being rich is no sin; just being poor is no virtue. We must understand that Jesus means the rich man is both wealthy and sinful—even evil. He has gained his wealth by corruption, by taking advantage of those with less ruthlessness. He has lied, stolen, attacked, and intimidated to get where he is. Lazarus, although the poorest of the poor, is also a man of faith. But we must also affirm that there are righteous wealthy people and really bad poor ones. In Jesus's day and time, however, one usually became wealthy by corrupt and abusive means.

I once attended an inner-city church. Most of the congregants that day were street people. They were dirty, smelly, and ragged. But at one point in the service, while Communion was being offered, a man rose and sang "Amazing Grace" along with the organ music. He had salt-and-pepper hair, stubble on his face, and wore a tattered wool jacket. His face and hands were dirty. He just stood up from his pew, evidently uninvited, and sang the hymn at the top of his lungs. His faith had overwhelmed him, and he could not hold it back. Every time I think of Lazarus, I see that man. I think that's what Jesus meant by Lazarus and that's what Jesus meant when he said, "Blessed are you poor, for yours is the kingdom of God" (Luke 6:20). These are the poor-yet-righteous.

Most of us who live in Europe or North America reside in a protective bubble. We are not used to suffering and poverty. And when it smacks us in the face, we withdraw from it, shrink back from it, ignore it. We step over it, so to speak, even as the rich man stepped over Lazarus and ignored him. Visiting developing countries helps us enter reality, helps us to see the other colors of the shoe, we might say. Walking through a downtown area of an urban center might help too. The number of beggars on the sidewalks of most American cities is staggering. Then, too, sometimes life just intrudes itself into our bubble-paradise. Someone we love gets sick or suffers in some way. Then we realize that we had been living a fantasy. We had looked at our fantasy world and had seen one color shoe; the majority of humanity always saw the other color.

So, what is this parable saying to us?

First, don't be oblivious to suffering. Don't hide your eyes or turn your head. The church is the last place where one would expect that to happen, but often it does. I hear stories all the time of Christian ministers who refuse to visit sick people or persons experiencing grief from the death of a loved one. A lady told me that, after her husband became bedfast due to a stroke, her pastor visited him exactly one time in fifteen years—only after she repeatedly begged him to come. Another man, whose mother had just died, received a phone call from his pastor. The minister said he could not come to his house to pray with him in his time of loss since being in the company of grieving persons upset him too much. A member of a midsize church reported that his minister never made hospital calls because hospitals "depressed" him. I don't mean to pick on the ministers here, but I think if the spiritual leaders have these attitudes, the members will likely have them as well. We just want to stay in our bubble. But Jesus is saying in this parable: "Don't hide your eyes from Lazarus. Don't just step over him."

Take some action. Donate money to a charity helping the suffering and sick. Volunteer to work in an agency or ministry. Take a mission trip to a poor country. Take action. Also, you might want to watch more than one television news station. Some of them just do not report on the suffering in this world.

Second, don't love "the show" more than the people. One pastor of a megachurch told me once, "I love the show." This man also refused to visit the sick and grieving. His sermons were full of the latest bells and whistles (glitzy PowerPoint shows to follow alongside his preaching). He often did what some called "stunts" during his sermons, things to call attention to himself in a showmanship kind of way.

But this loving-the-show and neglecting-the-suffering-of-human-beings I've heard of somewhere else, from a voice in the distant past. It is a good voice, a needed voice, both in its day and now in ours. The voice slowly rises in my ears and I hear the words:

> He who does not know Christ does not know God hidden in suffering. Therefore he prefers works to suffering, glory to the cross, strength to weakness, wisdom to folly . . . [but] God can be found only in suffering and the cross. . . . A theologian of glory . . . works to avoid suffering. And if he *is* afflicted with adversity, he concludes that he failed in his works.[2]

These are the words of Martin Luther. Five hundred years ago, Martin Luther criticized the church of his generation for its "Theology of Glory." These were church leaders and Christians who also loved the show. They loved ceremonies, pomp, dressing up, rituals, fame—in short, the show. Now these things are certainly not wrong. The problem is they are not at the heart of Christianity.

Luther instead pressed for a "Theology of the Cross." In this way of thinking and acting, Christ's suffering sensitizes us to the suffering of the world. The God of the cross speaks to us, for example, in the hiddenness of illness and poverty. We wonder why there is no miracle to cure the sick and restore prosperity to the poor but find instead, in God, a new strength to believe. This God, the authentic God of the Christian faith, hides himself in lowly things like a cross and human suffering. Our eyes cannot see him for the suffering, so we must exercise our faith. Sensitizing ourselves to suffering leads to authentic faith.

How ridiculous to celebrate and parade in church, putting on a show, and then close our eyes to the suffering of the world.

Christ suffered horribly but we act like, instead, he sang lead for a praise team at a megachurch and wore a sequined Elvis costume.

Third, have the mind of Christ when you encounter the poor, sick, grieving, and suffering. Jesus said:

> I was hungry and you gave me something to eat. I was thirsty and you gave me something to drink. I was a foreigner and you gave me hospitality. I was practically naked and you gave me clothes. I was sick and you took care of me. I was in prison and you came to me. . . . When you did it to one of these, the least of my brothers, you did it to me. (Matt. 25:35–40)

When you see a suffering person, see the face of Christ. When you hear of someone who is sick, think of it as if you are visiting our suffering Lord. When you reach out to comfort a grieving human being, consider it an act of ministering to Jesus on the cross.

I don't claim this is easy. Lazarus was not an enjoyable person to be with. I remember a time when a lady entered my office and burst into tears. She asked if I would come outside to the parking lot and talk with her husband. "My husband is in the car," she began. "Would you come out and talk to him? Nobody else will."

Thus began my acquaintance with this saintly, if unusual, couple that would continue for the next six months for him and the next few years for her. Later, as I stepped inside the door of their small frame house on the appointed day of my first visit, the wail arose almost immediately. The poor man was suffering from a terminal illness that had left him in terrible discomfort and pain. I won't describe the horrors of his condition. For the next hour, I listened in shocked silence to the most bone-chilling screams. He never stopped screaming! He knew his days were numbered and was begging God to take him immediately so he could escape his misery.

Finally, the howl died down, and after I prayed and as I was stumbling, dazed, out the door, I heard over my shoulder, "I feel better. Can you come back at the same time next week?" Until he died, I went through the weekly ordeal of listening to his wailing and begging for death.

Often, I groused on the way to his house, "If some preacher had done his job, I wouldn't have to endure this." But then I realized I was no better than the other guy. If I could have gotten out of this, I probably would have. Sometimes, I even had to bribe myself with the promise of a banana split or a walk in the park to motivate myself to return to the house of pain. Sometimes after those visits, I couldn't sleep at night.

Somehow, I endured, and around six months after my first encounter, I preached at his funeral. His four children were there, along with his widow and a few friends. They were all glowing in their thanks to me for ministering to their deceased loved one. They remarked about what a comfort my visits had been. I felt kind of ashamed since I really had not enjoyed them. I sometimes daydreamed about excuses to end the relationship. As I say, I was feeling ashamed about the whole experience. But then, no one ever said Lazarus was a fun guy. He was just—loved.

And he wore pink sneakers with white trim. Or were they gray with blue-green trim?

DISCUSSION QUESTIONS

1. Do you agree that this parable is really about what you see? What other themes are in the parable?

2. Are you tempted to walk away from street beggars? Is there a limit to the attitude Jesus taught in Matthew 5:42?

3. Why do we shy away from suffering and dying persons?

4. Does your church present a Theology of Glory or a Theology of the Cross? How can you tell the difference?

GOING DEEPER

The reference to Lazarus's being carried by the angels to Abraham's "bosom" or chest pictures a banquet scene like that of John 13:23, where the Beloved Disciple reclines and rests his head on Jesus's chest. In Roman banquets, diners reclined on the left elbow, three to a single couch. Thus, one "resting his head on someone's chest" meant he was eating next to him, reclining on the left elbow next to him. The person reclining next to the master of the feast (as the Beloved Disciple did next to Jesus in John 13:23) is in a place of honor. Since we presume Abraham is the master of the heavenly banquet, Lazarus is in the most honored place in paradise.[3]

The expression "bosom of Abraham" is found in Jewish literature. In a rabbinic work, it narrates the story of a mother exhorting her sons to stay loyal to their faith in the face of persecution. During the war against Emperor Hadrian led by Bar-Kokhba (AD 132–135), a woman lost all seven of her sons. Each was threatened with death if he did not worship an idol. Their mother exhorted them to remain faithful to the Torah so that in the time to come they would be put in the bosom of Abraham.[4] Thus, the expression "to be in the bosom of Abraham" was equated with eternal reward.

The name Lazarus comes from the Hebrew Elàzar, which means "God helped." Jesus did not choose the name at random. Every villager hearing this story would immediately make this connection. Jesus leaves the rich man unnamed. He reverses the common practice. Usually, they would give the name of the rich and powerful, and the dirty and poor would not be noticed (as in the story below). Here it leaves out the rich man's name and gives the name of the poorest of the poor.

There is a similar story[5] (the same one I told you about in Chapter Two) in the rabbinic literature about a rich man, a tax collector named Bar Mayan, and a poor Bible scholar. Note in the rabbinic story, the rich man's name is given but not the poor scholar's. The rich man died and was given a glorious funeral. Work stopped throughout the city so the whole population could escort him to his grave. At the same time, the poor man had a very simple funeral and nobody took any notice of his death. His good friend complained to God and was given a vision of the afterlife. In it, Bar Mayan was standing on the bank of a stream and trying to get to the water to drink but was unable to do so. The poor man was in gardens of paradise full of flowing streams.[6] Evidently, Jesus took a common story—meant to warn the greedy rich—and adapted it for his special illustration. A lot of people were troubled by how the greedy rich seemed to "win" in this life while the righteous poor did not. The point of the rabbinic parable and of Jesus's teaching as well is that we are not seeing the reality. Don't be fooled. They do not really "win."

Notice, by the way, Jesus does not say the rich man is in hell. He says he went to "Hades" and was tormented in flames (vv. 23–24). In the Greek language, Hades was where the spirits of the dead went. The Jews took this term over from the Greeks and used it as the place where the dead are, whether in bad straits or not.[7] In the New Testament the word is used several times. It is often accompanied by the word *death*: "death and Hades" (Rev. 1:18; 6:8; 20:13, 14). Jesus declares that "the gates of Hades will not prevail" against the church (Matt. 16:18). In Peter's sermon in Acts 2, he states that God did not leave Jesus in Hades (Acts 2:27, 31), but raised him from the dead. So, Hades is not necessarily the place of punishment, though it may become a place of punishment for the unrighteous. The ultimate place of punishment is hell (Greek: *ge-enna*). In our story, Hades simply means that the rich man is in the abode of the dead and is being punished. Lazarus, however, is in a totally different destiny: Abraham's bosom.

Is this story supposed to inform us about what the dead evil people experience right now or is it a vision into the future, after the Great Judgment? Jesus does not say, and he gives no definitive picture about the "waiting places" of the dead. He does say clearly that there will be consequences in the afterlife and that those consequences are not based on what the world usually values. The world looked at the Rich Man and saw somebody who had everything. It saw a "winner." Jesus saw flames.

NOTES

[1] For example, see Kelsey Stewart, "Is This Shoe Pink or Gray? Eye Expert Explains Viral Photo, Why Your Friends Are Crazy," October 16, 2017, www.omaha.com/livewellnebraska/health/is-this-shoe-pink-or-gray-eye-expert-explains-viral/article_ec8e8746-b040-11e7-9dea-873af5c6fa02.html.

[2] Martin Luther, "Heidelberg Disputations of 1518," English translation at www.catchpenny.org/heidel.html#E021.

[3] Danker, *Greek-English Lexicon.*

[4] Pesikta Rabbati 43.

[5] J. Hagigah 2.2//j. Sanhedrin 2.23.

[6] Jeremias, *Parables.*

[7] Danker, *Greek-English Lexicon.*

11

THE HATERS, THE HURTING, THE HEARTLESS, AND THE HEROES

Luke 10:30–35

You've probably heard some of those half-humorous, but also in a way very serious, statements: "There are two kinds of people in the world . . ." They intend to give us a truth in the humor. Here are a few:

- There are two kinds of people in the world: the givers and the takers.
- There are two kinds of people in the world: those who do the work and those who take credit for the work.
- There are two kinds of people in the world: those who leave you feeling up and those who leave you feeling down.

And some even expand the list.

- There are three kinds of people in the world: those who make things happen, those who let things happen, and those who stand around wondering what just happened.

You get the picture. These jokes want to categorize humanity in a way that makes us smile. ("Yes, I know people like that.") They seek to clarify for us what we already kind of know from our experiences. That's what this parable does. In this parable, Jesus gives us a look into not two or three kinds of people, but four.

There are four kinds of people in this story:

1. The Haters
2. The Hurting
3. The Heartless
4. The Heroes

Jesus does this in other parables as well, some of which we discuss in this book. For example, the Four Soils (Chapter Five) and the Three Stewards (Chapter Eight). So, what he does in this parable, which we usually refer to as the Parable of the Good Samaritan, is a frequent kind of teaching for Jesus. Let's look at each type of person.

First, Jesus describes the Haters. A guy was traveling from Jerusalem to Jericho (about twenty miles). He was probably a traveling, small-time merchant. He probably had a donkey loaded with his wares: maybe pottery, or brass pots and pans, or clothing. He intended to sell them in Jericho. All of a sudden, he is accosted by robbers.

Now the translation "robbers" is a little weak. This word is the one used for the armed and violent bandits that roamed the Roman Empire. They were vicious and deadly criminals. They often killed their robbery victims for no reason. Entire families might be wiped out. One story the ancients record for us is of a father and seven children who set out on a journey. They were all killed in a bandit attack, every one of them—even the kids. Throughout the territory of the former empire one can still see gravestones from the ancient world with the inscription "Killed by bandits." Enough said. Everyone knew what that meant. It happened all the time.

So, these brutal criminals attacked our victim as he traveled to make a few sales. He probably has a wife and five or six children back in Jerusalem. He can't afford to lose his donkey, his wares, and certainly not his life. Who will take care of the family? But the bandits do not care. They attack, steal everything he has—his donkey, his wares, even his clothes ("We can sell his clothes for a couple of bucks," they thought.)—and then beat the daylights out of him, intending to kill him. These were not nice people.

What makes people become haters? That I cannot answer. It may be a long process. But I do know that we have many haters in our contemporary society. Witness the number of mass shootings in the United States in recent years based on hate:

- Las Vegas, where a sniper killed more than fifty persons from a hotel window.
- The Emanuel AME church in Charleston, South Carolina, where a young man murdered nine persons just because they were Black.
- Virginia Beach, Virginia, at a municipal building where a man gunned down twelve souls.
- The El Paso, Texas, shooting in which twenty-two passed away, killed because they were Mexican.

And this is only a very partial list! Why did they do it? I do not know why. But we have a lot of hatred in our society right now. We live in a toxic world.

We do not need, however, to look only at these mass murderers for examples of haters. We hear it and see it almost constantly in the media. We live in a poisonous environment of verbal abuse, incivility, and insults. Why do people troll others on Twitter? Why do teenagers bully others on Facebook? We hear regularly that some preteen or teenager has committed suicide, unable to tolerate the bullying. What would make a person so hateful as to drive a kid to that end? Haters. The book of Proverbs said it well: "A fool's tongue is a scorching fire" (16:27). Folks, don't be a fool. Clean up your online life.

Please, God, may I never be a hater. If I am unknowingly, may I be shown so I can change.

Next are the Hurting. So, the poor guy is beaten to within an inch of his life and left "half-dead." They even took his clothes. He is now covered only by his own blood. He has cracked ribs, a concussion, a broken jaw, maybe a broken collarbone or arm. He is a mess. He has lost all his wares and his donkey. He hasn't even any clothes to wear to return home—if, indeed, he lives long enough to return home.

We have a lot of people walking around like that. They are hurting. I began ministry at age twenty-two. Soon thereafter, I was married and settled in for what I was sure would be absolutely enjoyable. I pictured myself preaching sermons, the congregation standing spontaneously at the end of each sermon, and hearing thunderous applause as I modestly marched down the aisle to the back of the church at the end of the service. Okay, that did not happen. What did happen was all the visits to my office and the phone calls—often in the middle of the night—to talk about problems. After I had been at this church about a year, I rose one Sunday to preach and the thought struck me: I've counseled with more than half of these people about their problems. What's wrong with this group? Are they abnormal? I eventually grew up a bit and concluded that they were not abnormal; they were just people. We are all wounded.

Later on, when I began teaching, I thought I would deliver brilliant theological lectures to standing ovations at the end of every class. (I keep having these delusions of grandeur.) But I quickly found that another dynamic developed. Students would come to my office, ask if they could shut the door, sit down, and begin crying. They told me about abusive homes and parents. Some of the parents had told these young people that they had never wanted them, that they thought the kids were losers, and that they didn't care if they ever saw them again. That kind of thing really leaves a scar on an eighteen-year-old. It's hard for them to think about theological issues when they are that damaged.

Chances are many of you reading this now have been hurt deeply. Some event, some person, some illness—something—has hurt you really badly. You feel scarred for life. You feel like you can never get over it and get past it.

I heard about a person who was really at the end of his emotional rope. Kevin Hines decided, on September 25, 2000, that he would walk to the middle of the Golden Gate Bridge and jump off. He just could not take whatever in his life was tormenting him. But he sort of left the door open just a crack. He said to himself, "If even one person today is kind to me, I won't jump."

He jumped. How sad that he could not find one person to be nice to him that day. Hurting people. They are all around us, and we often do not know it. That rude person in the checkout line might be really wounded. That driver full of road rage might be at her wit's end. You never know what is going on with people.

I want to say to you, if you are hurting, three things. First, you are not alone. Many more understand than you think. Others reading this have the same hurts as you. They want to help. Please reach out and tell someone about your problems. You may not find that kind person immediately, but they are there. And, remember, God is there. God sees your pain and he cares. You are not alone.

Second, your dark valley will pass. It may take some time. It may take some counseling. It may take a new direction in your life. But it will pass. Maybe it will not go away tomorrow or next month—even next year—but it will be gone someday.

Third, try to let the hurts go. Try to find forgiveness in your heart (see Chapter Four). Chances are that if you are passing through a dark tunnel right now, someone played a role in it. They either caused it or intensified it. Often natural causes brought a person to the point of desperation, but then some other person kicked them while they were down. Usually, no matter the source of the problem, another person has played some role. I hope you can reread Chapter Four and find a way to forgive.

Next, we have the Heartless. The poor guy is lying on the "road" (actually more like a hiking trail for us), and two religious leaders walk right by him. First the priest and then the Levite walk on by. One commentator suggests, plausibly, that they had just come from their one-week duty in the temple and were on their way home.[1] Not only do they walk past him; they walk as far away from him as they can ("on the other side"). They were evidently concerned about contracting ritual impurity. The Old Testament prohibited priests from having contact with a corpse. They evidently thought the poor guy was dead. We kind of understand them. They were bound by the rules of their calling. But the problem is they let their religious obligations interfere with human compassion, an absolute no-no for Jesus. In the Gospels, Jesus repeatedly puts more emphasis on compassion than rituals, rules, or customs (e.g., Mark 2:23–27; John 9:1–16). The core of Jesus's ethic is compassion (love for God and neighbor). Everything else takes second place.

You see, there are always somewhat valid reasons for not helping someone:

- I couldn't help that guy on the road because I was late for church. Don't you believe in church attendance?
- I can't go into that place to minister to people because I don't associate with crowds like that. Do you?
- Don't ask me for help while I'm praying.
- I don't give to street beggars because I never know how they will use the two dollars. Do you want me to encourage drug use?
- These people are here illegally. I don't help people like that. Do you want me to flout the law?

The priest and Levite were not evil guys. They were just bound to their calling. Why did Jesus make them the heartless? Because even a very good thing like God's calling to ministry can become an excuse to refuse kindness. We can fool ourselves that the neglect of a need is necessary for a higher, more spiritual principle. Wow!

But sometimes the heartlessness is evil and intentional. The heartlessness in our world often stuns us. After every disaster—tsunamis, hurricanes, floods, fires—fake websites spring up claiming to raise money for the victims. Of course, these fakes are only raising money for themselves. They take money needed for suffering people and redirect it to their corrupt bank accounts. They may make emotional appeals by telephone, "Please, can you help these poor children? They are really in trouble." But they will pocket every dime you give. Heartless.

In 2017, a most shocking example of heartlessness appeared on the news. Five teenage boys watched, videoed, and mocked a drowning man. It took him several minutes to drown. He had overturned a boat on a lake and, since he could not swim, was splashing in horror and trying to stay afloat. The boys laughed at the "funny" predicament the man had gotten himself into. They even hurled insults at the man as he died. He was stupid, they said, for getting himself into this situation.[2] Heartless.

One of the most heartbreaking examples of this mindset happens every time we have a mass shooting. Parents of children killed in schools and other relatives of mass shooting victims report that they often, themselves, receive death threats. The heartless threateners do not like having people on television claiming their child or spouse was killed by a shooter. They threaten to kill the people talking about these events. They claim the mass shootings are all made up. Terrible. These victims are twice hurt. First, their loved one is gunned down. Then, they are forbidden under threat of death themselves from expressing their grief.

What makes people so heartless? It is a spiritual sickness, an emptiness of the soul.

But then we have the Heroes. The Samaritan comes along, and everything changes. He could have just gone on, but heroes don't do that. He could have said, "He's not from my ethnic group. I only help people from my race and ethnic group." But heroes don't talk that way. He could have said, "Why should I spend my money on a stranger?" But heroes don't have that attitude. He could have thought, "I don't want to get involved. It will take time and effort that I don't have." But heroes take time.

Once more in his parables (in verse 33), Jesus used the Greek word *splagchnizomai,* "to show compassion."[3] We saw it already in Chapters One and Four, but used there in reference to God. This is one of the few places in Jesus's teaching where he attributes this strong emotion of compassion to a human being. And the Samaritan has it! The hated Samaritan acts like God. He imitates God.

Jesus made the hero a Samaritan, someone not quite Jewish. Although the Samaritans were the remnants of the northern tribes of Israel, they and the Jews (remnants of the tribe of Judah) had a history of hostility and violence toward each other. I might compare their animosity to that of the Catholics and Protestants in Northern Ireland. The two groups are the same basic religion (Christian) and are both Irish, but have different religious histories and customs and a shared memory of violence. That can make for hard feelings for generations. Likewise, the Jews and Samaritans were basically Israelites in religion and race, but their religious observances had separated from one another a bit since the Exile, and they had an unfortunate history of animosity and sometimes violence.

But this Samaritan did not see a Jew; he saw a human being who was hurting. As the old poem goes:

> He drew a circle that shut me out;
> heretic, rebel, a thing to flout.
> But love and I had the wit to win;
> we drew a circle that took him in. (Edwin Markham)

Heroes stop. They suffer inconvenience. They give a few bucks to homeless beggars. They listen to people's troubles. They stop.

Heroes are healers. They know the tremendous healing power of love. Dr. Karl Menninger wrote, "Love has awesome power. It cures people, both those who give it and those who receive it." Dear reader, be a hero.

In May 2019, tornado sirens went off in St. Louis, Missouri. Cars were driving furiously to get home before the potential disaster struck. Among the traffic was a man in a wheelchair, Gregory Beck. Beck is a double amputee and legally blind. One eye is completely blind and he has only partial sight in the other. He too was hurrying as fast as he could push his wheelchair. But from where he was, it would take him at least twenty-five minutes. Meanwhile, cars were honking at him to get out of their way. They drove on by him and yelled at him. It was a time of panic. But as a mother and sixteen-year-old son passed by, the son—Seth Phillips—asked his mother to stop. The boy hopped out and pushed Gregory Beck home. Imagine how Gregory felt to be cared for in that way.[4] Heroes.

In May of 2019, we heard of two more heroes: Riley Howell and Kendrick Castillo. Both gave their lives to save the lives of others. They were young, early twenties and a teenager. Each young man, you see, rushed a shooter, a person intending to commit mass murder. Howell was on a college campus (UNC Charlotte), and Castillo was in a high school in Colorado. Their selfless heroism saved the lives of others. They tackled the shooters, dying in the process, to allow the other students to escape. No heartlessness there. Heroes.

Sandy and Lonnie Phillips have a full-time job. They live in a camper and travel from mass shooting to mass shooting to minister to and comfort the survivors. They, unfortunately, keep very busy doing this. They receive no pay. They just do it. You see, they know that kind of grief firsthand. Their daughter was killed in 2012 in the Aurora, Colorado, shooting. They were crushed by her death. But now they are trying to turn their loss and pain into a way to help others. They travel the country hoping to build a network of survivors to offer victims and families comfort.[5] Often the deepest hurts lead to the greatest heroes.

Remember that guy, Kevin Hines, who jumped off the Golden Gate Bridge? Only about one percent survive that jump. He was in that number. He broke many bones but lived. Today, he works in suicide prevention. He is trying to turn his suffering into heroism.[6] On the day he jumped, he couldn't find even one person to be kind to him. Now he wants to be the kind person who prevents someone else from jumping. Often the deepest hurts lead to the greatest heroes.

That's our challenge. Stop; lift up the fallen; bind up the wounded; show compassion. Be a hero.

DISCUSSION QUESTIONS

1. What do you think makes people become haters?

2. Making the Samaritan the hero is a surprise ending. Why do you think Jesus made the hero a Samaritan? Why did he make the religious leaders the heartless?

3. We see many movies today (especially the *Avengers* films) that feature superheroes. These are people with superpowers, some of whom do good and others who do evil. Why do we not celebrate those with moral superpowers?

4. Have you suffered a deep hurt? If you are recovering, how have you managed it?

GOING DEEPER

The Jews and the Samaritans had a history of violence. Jews from Galilee would regularly cut through Samaria on their way to Jerusalem for a feast. The local Samaritan villagers did not like having crowds of people pass through their land. (A similar thing happened in Jesus's ministry; Luke 9:51–56.) Sometimes violence would erupt and even lead to bloodshed. When that happened, the side aggrieved would seek revenge, and then the violence would be ramped up. Josephus, the Jewish historian from the first century AD, tells of such cases (*Jewish War* 2.232–235). In this story, the Samaritan villagers killed some Jews from Galilee on their way to Passover. The Jews appealed to the Roman procurator for justice. The procurator refused. The Jews then asked a notorious bandit to help. The bandit pillaged and killed people in several villages in Samaria.

Bandits were very bad people who terrorized travelers—both rich and poor—and who preyed upon local farmers throughout the Roman Empire for centuries before and after the ministry of Jesus. So widespread was the phenomenon that Ulpian's *Digest* of Roman law (13.6.5) lists old age, sickness, and bandits as the common causes of death. Death at the hands of bandits is even classed alongside storms, fire, and earthquakes as death by natural causes (*Digest* 13.6.18). Paul also (2 Cor. 11:26) alludes to the dangers of travel due to violent bandits. He writes that he often traveled in danger of bandits. It was not uncommon for a person to set out on a journey and never be seen or heard of again.

The bandits often killed their victims. Throughout the region known in antiquity as the Roman Empire one can still see tombstones from that time with the inscription "Killed by bandits." One historian collected scores of these inscriptions from all over the empire. Enough said; it was a common way to die in the ancient world. Sometimes entire families, including children, were just wiped out by roving gangs of bandits like the ones in our parable (see above). An inscription commemorates the death of a ten-year-old girl who was murdered by bandits just because she wore jewelry.[7] These bandits were young men (and are almost always men) between the ages of thirteen and twenty who, because of poverty, landlessness, or, simply, boredom from living on the farm, pursued the "exciting" life of killing and pillaging. We should picture the attackers in our parable as teenagers who have learned the ethos and skills to murder.

Leviticus 21:1–3 commands that priests may not contract "corpse uncleanness"—that is, have any contact with a dead body except for their close family members. That meant that he could not touch a corpse, be in the same room or house as a corpse, or even bend over a corpse (Num. 19:16). This is the scripture text that the priest and Levite were obeying.

NOTES

[1] Foster, *Studies in the Life of Christ.* Priests and Levites served in the temple for one week at a time, twice a year. The rest of the time, they usually returned to their home village somewhere in Judea.

[2] Nick Valencia and Devon Sayers, "Florida Teens Who Recorded Drowning Man Will Not Be Charged in His Death," *CNN*, July 21, 2017, www.cnn.com /2017/07/20/us/florida-teens-drowning-man/index.html.

[3] See Chapter One.

[4] Madeline Holcombe, "Drivers Honked as a Man in a Wheelchair Raced Home during a Storm. This Teen Stopped to Push Him All the Way," *CNN*, May 25, 2019, www.cnn.com/2019/05/25/us/st-louis-wheelchair-storm-teen -trnd/index.html.

[5] Survivors Empowered, www.survivorsempowered.org, accessed January 31, 2020.

[6] Kevin Hines, www.kevinhinesstory.com, accessed January 31, 2020.

[7] Brent Shaw, "Bandits in the Roman Empire," *Past & Present* 105 (1984): 3–52.

12

THE GOLDEN BOY

Luke 15:25–32

In the summer of 2008, I helped with an archaeological excavation at the site of ancient Cana, the village where Jesus performed his first miracle. The ruin lies on a low hill overlooking a large, flat valley (called the Beit Netofa Valley). This particular summer, they had planted mostly watermelons in the valley, along with a few rows of corn. It was nearing the time of the watermelon harvest, so many landowners of this fertile valley were camping near their crop to protect against theft. Just below the ruins of Cana was one such family living in a long, rectangular tent. They evidently observed us excavating up on the hill every day and wanted to show some typical Arab hospitality. So, they sent someone up one day, a friend who spoke a little English, to invite us for fresh watermelon after the day's work. We arrived at the tent in midafternoon to be officially greeted. The women were hidden behind a curtain in the tent. We could hear them giggling as they peeked at us through the cracks in the curtain. Standing at attention at the other end of the tent were the father of the family and his oldest son. We were supposed to greet them by shaking hands and then help ourselves to a slice of watermelon. So, we approached and each of us shook the hands of the owner and the heir. Standing behind the two was the younger son. Now, I am a Christian pastor, so I shake hands with everyone, out of habit. After shaking the father's hand and that of the oldest son, I reached around to shake the hand of the second son. When I did, the father made a face and hand motion as if to say, "Don't bother with that one."

In that moment, I understood a lot about this parable. In Middle Eastern culture, the oldest son is the prince of the family. All other children are second class, so to speak. The younger sons are spare parts in case something happens to the oldest son. The daughters are more of a burden than a source of family pride. All the family's dreams and hopes for the future are invested in the oldest son. We should think of this parable in that context.

We need to remember the occasion for this parable, or actually, the second half of a parable. (We talked about the first part of the parable in Chapter One.) At the beginning of Luke chapter 15, Jesus is associating—eating with—tax collectors (that is, mafia-like figures who engage in extortion) and "sinners" (who are thieves, cutthroats, prostitutes, swindlers, and drunks). Jesus's association with these bad people causes the Pharisees and the scribes to level strong criticism against him. "Why would anybody hang out with such bad people?" was probably what the Pharisees thought. It was a question they asked more than once as they observed Jesus's ministry (Luke 5:30, 7:39). In response to this criticism, Jesus told the parable of the lost sheep, the lost coin, and the lost younger son. In each of these parables, the thing lost represents the tax collectors and sinners—the bad persons.

But now, in a sort of appendix to the parable of the prodigal or lost younger son, Jesus adds the story of the older brother/older son. This person represents the Pharisees and scribes. At this point, we realize something very surprising. The father of the parable had two sons, and *both* of them were lost. It's like the classic movie called *The Sixth Sense,* in which the little boy says, "I see dead people, and they don't know they're dead." In Jesus's last parable—in the appendix to his greatest parable we know about—he is saying, "I see lost people, and they don't know they're lost." These Pharisees and scribes[1] don't know they are also lost, just like the tax collectors and sinners.

This last parable is a challenge to all of us. The father had *two* sons: the blatant sinner and the bitterly resentful, coldhearted good citizen. As we seek to apply the story to the modern church, we should recognize that in the church there are two categories of Christians: the new converts and the lifetime Christians; that is, those who have come to faith as adults—sometimes after a really rough or bad period—and those who have grown up in the church. The challenge is for us to ask, "Which one am I, and how does this affect my perspective on being a Christian?"

When I think about this second half of the Parable of the Prodigal Son, I see the older son as *entitled*, or as thinking that he was entitled. He was the prince of the family. He was the golden boy. Had he been in a modern American high school, he would have been the captain of the football team and the president of the student council. He would have been winsome and handsome. The girls would have swooned over him. This son has always done right, has always succeeded. He has also always been the center of attention. He cannot understand failure and he cannot comprehend weakness. He has no patience for either. He also cannot tolerate competition for honor and attention.

Many in our churches are "older brother" Christians. I myself am one. I pretty much grew up in the church. I can't remember *not* attending church. I know the lingo, the unspoken rules and expectations, and which behaviors are considered inappropriate. I know these things just by osmosis. I am an "older brother" Christian.

There is, of course, nothing wrong with that. The problem can be that we become proud of our outward righteousness but lack submission of the heart. Son number one, the older brother, had served the father outwardly ("I worked for you many years and never transgressed any of your commandments!" v. 29). He has served out of duty and obligation, but he does not seem to love his father. He thought that since he had served his father faithfully, he ought to get something out of it. His service was transactional, reciprocal. His complaint was, "What do *I* get out of this? You never gave *me* a goat to have a banquet with *my* friends!" It's as if he's asking, "What was all my work for if you're going to give parties to that wild kid and neglect me?" Transactional.

I love the quotation by John Piper, the retired pastor: "The gospel is not the way to get to heaven. It is the way to get to God." The point is, we should follow the gospel because it will lead us closer to God and not because of what we will get out of it. To do the latter is to act out of selfish motives. I am sure Piper believes in heaven, but making heaven the main motive for serving God is a kind of spiritual transactionalism. Many "older brother" Christians are following the gospel almost entirely because it will lead to heaven. It's like a young man proposing to his girlfriend and having her reply: "Well, I don't love you, but how much money do you have in the bank?" Transactional Christians' love for God is questionable.

The older brother (son number one) was, in his way, just as self-centered as the prodigal son, the wild and wayward child. The younger son wanted his pleasure and fun and did not care how he hurt his father to get it. It was all about *his* pleasure. But Christians of duty and obligation—"older brother" Christians—can be just as ego driven as pleasure-seeking sinners. We are in it for our own benefit and not because we love God. We feel obligated to earn our reward and are willing to take up the burden of obedience for a deferred time of pleasure and fun.

My mother died in 2011. She was eighty-seven years old when she passed. She was healthy and aware until the last couple of years. But in those latter days, I often worried about her health and her well-being. I made more frequent visits to look in on her. I worried that she might fall (and she did); I worried that she was not eating properly; I worried that she was forgetting to take her meds. Now during that time, suppose all I talked about was the inheritance I would someday gain from her will. Suppose I kept saying to friends and other family members, "I just can't wait to get that inheritance! I'm really going to enjoy spending it." What would people have—rightly—thought? They would have thought that I didn't really care for my mother at all but that I only wanted what I would gain from my attentiveness. Transactional. The truth is, I should care for my mother just because she is my mother, whether she has any wealth to leave me or not. Likewise, Christians should love God just because he is God. The medieval preacher Bernard of Clairvaux wrote: "God is not loved without reward, though he should be loved without regard for one."

There is a great song out now, sung by Natalie Grant, that captures this thinking.[2] It says that God can, of course, take away every pain, every problem, and every heartache in a second. But even if he doesn't, we should want God just because he is God. We should want God for who he is and not for what he will give us. In the song, she prays that she will want the Healer more than the healing, the Savior more than the saving, and the Giver more than the giving. Yes, that's the idea. We should want God just because he is God, whether we get anything from him or not.

In addition to being self-centered, the older brother was *hateful.* Listen to how he speaks about his little brother: "When this son *of yours* comes . . ." He doesn't say "my brother," but "this son of yours." He doesn't go into the party to inquire about the health and well-being of his brother. He has no interest in seeing his brother. The little brother, the prodigal son, could easily have been killed. I picture the prodigal as a teenager (see Chapter One). I surmise that we should think of him as around fifteen or sixteen. Picture this kid walking into a large gentile city with a bag of money under his armpit and asking, "Where's the fun?" He could easily have been knocked in the head, had his throat cut, or otherwise been ill-used. Many young persons have left on such sow-your-wild-oats trips and have never come back. Yet the older brother does not express interest in his younger brother's welfare. He doesn't even ask the servant about him: "Does he have an eye or a hand missing? Is he half-dead from starvation or disease?" The servant announces briefly that the kid is in good health (v. 27). But that could mean many things. Of good health but missing a foot? Running a high fever but otherwise he looks good? He asks no such questions—nothing.

The older brother seems jealous of the attention now directed at the prodigal. The older brother is supposed to be the prince, the heir, and the golden boy. The attention should be his, not this wayward wild kid's. The older brother has become Cain to his little brother's Abel. In this Genesis 4 story, Cain, out of jealousy, rises up and murders his brother Abel. This older kid sounds like he could almost do the same. His response to his father is full of rage (v. 28) at the attention focused on the little brother, the prodigal, the wild child. He stands outside and fumes. Rage.

Let's face it, new converts can be a bother. And when they have come out of drugs, prison, prostitution, or other unsavory backgrounds, the "older brother" Christians do not know how to react. The new converts have rough edges. They don't know the vocabulary of the church and don't know the unspoken rules. I recall one such person way back in one of my ministries. He was in his mideighties and had lived a rather rough life. He was cantankerous and set in his ways, but trying to learn what it meant to be a Christian. The first Sunday after his baptism, it was time for his first Communion. The Communion trays were passed to him and he didn't know exactly what to do. We had failed to explain it. We just assumed everyone knew what to do because almost all of us were "older brother" Christians. This stuff is like breathing for us. It just comes naturally because we have done it all our lives. Well, he fumbled around a little and eventually dropped the cup on his lap and spilled the contents on his pants . . . whereupon he did what he had always done: he unleashed a tirade of profanity which the entire church heard. Very embarrassing for him and really for all of us. New converts are a bother.

Regular members can ask, "Who needs these newcomers? They just make trouble." Sometimes the irritation is when the newcomers are poor or of a different ethnic group. They have strange ways and behaviors. They may speak a different language and only understand English marginally. Trouble.

Sometimes the problem is that the new Christian is from such a bad background. The "older brother" Christians cannot understand how anybody that bad could reform. "The leopard does not change his spots" becomes their knee-jerk response. Here's the thing: people cannot understand the power of true repentance if they have never really repented themselves. Many of us "older brother" Christians who grew up in the church never really had a repentance crisis. We have never been broken by our sin and, consequently, we can't understand what the new Christians have experienced. Can anybody really change that much? Absolutely! But the older brothers among us have difficulty grasping that, and this difficulty makes us suspicious of the new converts.

Furthermore, the older brother was *disrespectful* toward his father. He wouldn't even go into the house to attend the father's party. And when he speaks to his father (v. 29–30), I hear him screaming at him. He is filled with rage that the father has forgiven the younger brother, has taken him back, and has even thrown the wild kid a party! And so, the older brother talks ugly to his father. He has no concern that his father has spent sleepless nights and stressful days worrying over his second son. How many days did the father climb to the rise of the nearest hill in hope of seeing the head of his prodigal appear on the horizon? How many times did he wake up in the night thinking he heard the voice of the teenager, hoping he had heard his voice, the voice of his beloved child? But the older brother apparently has had no concern for the father's grief. And now that the father is weak with relief, the older son is only angry. Disrespectful.

The older brother is nothing like his father. His father is a loving, forgiving, generous man. But the older brother is petty, jealous, unforgiving, and unyielding. Who is the real disgrace and shame of the family? Is it the prodigal brother or the jealous and petty brother? This man had two sons, and both of them were lost.

We "older brother" Christians must learn this truth: If God loves sinners, who are we to reject them? When we enter heaven someday, we may be surprised at God's generosity. Be more like God and rejoice that sinners have been saved. They were once lost and now are found; they were dead and are now alive.

William Paul Young is the author of the international best seller *The Shack*. He now has a book out called *Lies We Believe about God*. In this book, he tells a sort of parable of his own. In the story, people have died and are approaching the pearly gates of heaven. Standing at the gates is Peter, the great apostle. The first guy asks Peter if he may enter. Peter tells him that he needs a hundred points. This guy thinks that's pretty easy in light of all he's done in the church. He lists working in the church's soup kitchen and helping the poor for fifteen years. Peter says he gets one point for all that. The guy starts to panic. Only one point for all that? Then the same guy reports that he is a Christian pastor and has preached and ministered for thirty-five years. Again, Peter says he will award one point for all that. Now the guy realizes that he only has two points after all those years of service and work. He is really in a panic. Then he sees a man from the town where he pastored a church for many years. This man came to church mostly on Christmas and Easter. He seemed like a nice enough guy but just never got into church work much. Surprisingly, this second man just waves at Peter and walks right into heaven. The first guy is angry and scandalized. Can this second man really have a hundred points for that? Peter's reply is a classic: "Oh no, he just doesn't play this game."

And that's the problem. Many of us "older brother" Christians do play the game. In the game, if you earn enough points, you win. We are out there earning points from a God we think is in a transactional relationship with us. We serve out of duty but not out of love. In love, I would help my mother whether she has any money to bequeath to me or not. In love, we would want Jesus more than anything, whether he takes away our pains and burdens or not. But we are operating on obligation. We are the modern Pharisees and scribes.

This father had two sons: both were lost. But here's the interesting part. We know the fate of the younger brother, the wild kid. He repented; he changed. We are not told what happened to the older brother. His story is still open.

The longer we have been "in the faith," the more easily we fall into the older brother mentality. We are entitled; we are special to God. The older brother in this story and the Pharisee who went up to pray (Chapter Six) are warnings to all of us who "trust in our own righteousness."

DISCUSSION QUESTIONS

1. Are you a prodigal Christian or an "older brother" Christian? In other words, were you raised in the church or did you come to faith later in life? How do you think your biography has affected your understanding of the gospel of grace?

2. What do you think about the idea that we should not find our primary motive for Christian obedience in the hope for heaven? Do you agree that having heaven as your main reason for being a Christian is ego driven and transactional?

3. Do you think "older brother" Christians are sometimes jealous of the attention new converts receive?

4. Do you think the new converts, the prodigal Christians, sometimes fail to appreciate the stability and service that the "older brother" Christians bring to church life?

GOING DEEPER

We should imagine that the father in the story was the owner of a large estate. He would have been in the one-thousand-acre category: he had slaves to do his bidding at every moment (vv. 22–23, 26). This size estate in first-century Palestine was considered quite large. In Palestine at this time, an estate of between 50 and 300 acres was a medium-sized estate. One could live "like a gentleman" on only about one hundred acres. That is, you did no actual work yourself. You had agricultural workers and a farm manager to do the work. You just kind of loafed. A gentleman does not work.

I calculate, however, that this family was in the large estate class (over 300 acres). The family was very wealthy by the standards of that day. The largest estates in Palestine at this time that we know of were around twice that large. These were owned by the Herodian family. Therefore, those of somewhat lesser size were owned by the nonroyal aristocrats like our family in the parable.[3]

When the father divided up the estate, the older brother would have gotten a double share (Deut. 21:17). Thus, he would have received around 650 acres, while the younger son would have received around 350 acres. A farm of 350 acres in antiquity made a person a gentleman, as noted above, and even put him in the large estate category. The younger son could have had a comfortable lifestyle on his land had he retained it. He would have had all his wants satisfied with absolutely no effort on his part. But he wanted excitement and adventure. Was he like the bandits I described in the previous chapter who left home in their teenage years because they were bored with life on the farm?

Evidently, the younger son has sold his share of the estate and taken the money. The buyer would now be the owner of the 350 acres but could not have the crops on it (the usufruct) until the father's death. Likewise, the older son now has the ownership of his share (two-thirds), while the father retains the "usufruct" or the right to the harvest of the land until his death (v. 12; he "divided up to them his estate").

When the older brother complains that he has worked many years for the father, he uses a verb that means literally "slaved for many years" (v. 29). He has worked very hard to make the estate pay off, while the younger brother has not worked at all in the recent months (or years?). Most sons of wealthy landowners did not actually do physical labor. Did the father compel the sons to do manual labor to prepare them for adulthood? If so, the lessons did not take.

NOTES

[1] I don't mean to imply that all the Pharisees and scribes were lost. Here I am referring to these specific judgmental and uncompassionate ones. We Christians must use care to avoid painting groups with the same brush. See Chapter Six.

[2] Becca Mizell and Samuel Mizell, "More than Anything," sung by Natalie Grant, copyright © 2015 Maxx Melodies (SESAC) / BMG Platinum Songs (BMI) / Takin It to the Maxx (BMI). All Rights Administered By BMG Rights Management (US) LLC.

[3] See Fiensy, *The Social History of Palestine in the Herodian Period.*

EPILOGUE

There is a story about an American army colonel. He was a headstrong man who often refused to heed the advice of experts and others who might have wisdom to share. He insisted on going his own way and pushing the envelope, so to speak. His strong will and risk-taking personality helped him to advance up to a certain point. People considered him daring and dashing. The risks he took early in his career paid off. But eventually, that kind of folly leads to disaster.

The colonel's stubborn refusal to take advice propelled him toward his final, tragic defeat. He and all the men in his command were killed in battle. After the battle, two Cheyenne women claimed they went to the battlefield, found the body of this headstrong man, and drilled holes into his eardrums so he could hear better in the afterlife. This is the legacy of the famous George Armstrong Custer, the man who would not listen—not to the Native Americans, not to his commanding officers, not to his army scouts, and not to his military instruction manuals. He would not hear them.

Some persons just will not take advice and teaching. The admonition of Jesus in these parables is to pay attention, to learn, to open our minds to his message. That is why he was often heard to say, "Whoever has ears to hear, let him [or her] hear." I pray that you, reader, will take heed and will focus your attention on these parables and their message. And I hope that, after you have read this book and examined the twelve parables discussed in it, you will take the extensive list of parables given in the Introduction to this book and continue to study them with your friends. Let this book be the beginning of many more years of "hearing."

SELECT BIBLIOGRAPHY

Bailey, Kenneth. *Jesus through Middle Eastern Eyes.* Downers Grove, IL: InterVarsity Press Academic, 2008.

———. *Poet and Peasant and through Peasant Eyes: A Literary-Cultural Approach to the Parables of Luke.* Grand Rapids: Eerdmans, 1983.

Blomberg, Craig L. *Interpreting the Parables.* Downers Grove, IL: InterVarsity Press, 1990.

Capon, Robert Farrar. *Kingdom, Grace, Judgment: Paradox, Outrage, and Vindication in the Parables of Jesus.* Grand Rapids: Eerdmans, 2002.

Connick, C. Milo. *Jesus the Man, the Mission, and the Message.* Edgewood Cliffs, NJ: Prentice Hall, 1974.

Danker, Frederick William. *A Greek-English Lexicon of the New Testament and Other Early Christian Literature,* 3rd ed. Chicago: University of Chicago Press, 2000.

Fiensy, David A. *The Archaeology of Daily Life: Ordinary Persons in Late Second Temple Israel.* Eugene, OR: Cascade, 2020.

———. *The Message and Ministry of Jesus.* Lanham: University Press of America, 1996.

———. *The Social History of Palestine in the Herodian Period: The Land Is Mine.* Lewiston: Edwin Mellen, 1991.

Foster, R. C. *Studies in the Life of Christ.* Joplin, MO: College Press, 1995.

Hunter, Archibald M. *Interpreting the Parables.* Louisville: Westminster John Knox, 1976.

Jeremias, Joachim. *The Parables of Jesus.* New York: Charles Scribner's Sons, 1963.

Malina, Bruce J., and Richard L. Rohrbaugh. *Social-Science Commentary on the Synoptic Gospels.* Minneapolis: Fortress, 1992.

McArthur, Harvey K., and Robert M. Johnston. *They Also Taught in Parables: Rabbinic Parables from the First Centuries of the Christian Era.* Grand Rapids: Academie, 1990.

Scott, B. Brandon. *Hear Then the Parable.* Minneapolis: Fortress, 1990.

Snodgrass, Klyne. *Stories with Intent: A Comprehensive Guide to the Parables of Jesus.* Grand Rapids: Eerdmans, 2008.

Westermann, Claus. *The Parables of Jesus in the Light of the Old Testament.* Minneapolis: Fortress, 1990.